Kids' Skills

BEN FURMAN

Ben Furman is a psychiatrist, psychotherapist and a prolific writer whose books have been translated worldwide. He is codirector of the Helsinki Brief Therapy Institute and hosts his own psychology-related talk show on Finnish television. Ben is the creator of the innovative method for working with children known as Kids' Skills. He teaches and consults internationally on solution-focused therapy, problem solving, children's issues, team building, systems thinking and personal development.

Ben Furman

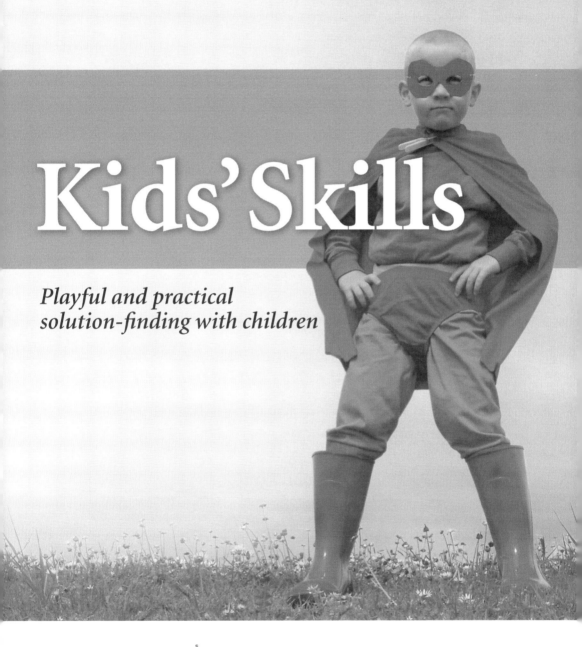

Kids' Skills

Playful and practical
solution-finding with children

St Luke's Innovative Resources

St Luke's Innovative Resources
137 McCrae Street
BENDIGO VIC 3550 Australia
Phone 03 5442 0500 International +61 3 5442 0500
Fax 03 5442 0555 International +61 3 5442 0555
info@innovativeresources.org
www.innovativeresources.org
ABN 99 087 209 729

First published in Finnish,
under the title *Muksuoppi,*
by Kustannusosakeyhtiö Tammi,
Helsinki 2003
First published in English
in Australia in 2004.

Reprinted in 2007

National Library of Australia
Cataloguing-in-Publication data:

Furman, Ben.
[Muksuoppi Finnish.]
Kids' skills: playful and practical
solution-finding with children.

English language ed.
ISBN 0 9580188 9 8

1. Child Development.
2. Emotions in children.
3. Children Health and hygiene.
I. Title.

155.4

Copy editing: Alan Simpson
Project management: Karen Masman
Cover design: Brent Seamer
Page design and layout: brad@onedegree.com.au
Printing: McPherson's Printing Group
Victoria Australia

Foreword

A number of years ago, I was attending a professional conference—a meeting of 300 or so therapists who worked with children and families. There were scholarly presentations and lively (but serious) discussions about various aspects of counselling or therapy with children and families. I knew that the conference organisers had invited an overseas 'expert' to give the keynote address. I had heard of Dr Ben Furman; he was a renowned psychiatrist from Finland, and I was looking forward to finding out what I could learn from him.

I saw Ben Furman a number of times during that conference. Mostly, I saw him rushing to the tennis court or coming back excitedly from the tennis court. I also saw him eating, drinking, joking and laughing. This famous psychiatrist had been flown all the way from Europe to be the keynote speaker at a conference and what I saw him doing most was HAVING FUN!

In my own therapeutic work, I often say to parents and children, 'You need to be very careful of people like me!' When they look a little perplexed, I explain, 'Well, I spent a number of years at university learning how to make things much more complicated than they usually need to be.'

People look to experts to help them resolve their difficulties; experts who presumably know more and have the specialised knowledge that is required to deal with something too difficult for the 'ordinary' person to solve. Parents and teachers, faced with a child's problem that perplexes or troubles them, turn to the expert—often, not only for an answer, but also for an explanation and/or a diagnosis. Curiously, as soon as the problem goes to the expert, it becomes bigger, more serious and more complicated.

Billy's difficulty sitting still in class and following directions wanders aimlessly into the doctor's office and comes out transformed into Attention Deficit Hyperactivity Disorder (with the very impressive initials of ADHD). Amelia's feelings of being scared about going to school are coaxed gingerly and hesitantly into the counsellor's office and emerge a little while later with the new name of 'Separation Anxiety'.

If you didn't think you, as a parent or a teacher, could solve the problem of someone not sitting still, you certainly won't be able to solve a problem as impressive as ADHD. If Amelia was feeling scared and concerned (and perhaps a little embarrassed) by her worries about school, she will most likely feel completely powerless when she knows it's really some big-sounding psychiatric thing.

I should have realised, all those years ago, that when problems (and the children they took with them) ventured into the tennis-playing Dr Furman's office, they would most certainly not be ushered out with a new, important-sounding psychiatric name that just confirmed how serious they were. I should have known that problems (and the children and parents who tagged along with them) would most likely have a very different experience. Clearly, Ben Furman was seriously committed to having fun and the people who consulted him would also discover some serious fun.

The book you are reading is revolutionary and subversive. It is designed to put counsellors and psychologists and psychiatrists out of business. (Now I know why he spent so much time practising his tennis!) Have you ever noticed that when a child's problem gets taken to the doctor or the psychologist, somehow the child gets lost? Kids' Skills puts the kid back in centre stage. (And, yes, it's the kid. This is not about 'paediatrics', it's not about the niceties of childhood—this is about the reality of what kids can achieve.) Also, professional help usually focusses more and more on 'getting to the bottom of what's wrong' (which is hardly encouraging). Kids' Skills begins by looking at what the kid can learn, build and develop.

Ben Furman says that Kids' Skills, 'forces us to re-examine the way we cooperate with children'. Ben begins from the premise that we can cooperate with children in resolving the behavioural, emotional and so-called psychiatric problems they present. This is not simply a tricky way for professionals to 'engage' children. Rather, it is a simple program that reflects a fundamental belief that children can learn skills to overcome even seemingly serious problems.

Kids' Skills gives solutions back to kids—and to their parents and teachers and youth leaders. It has nothing to do with 'being positive' but is a simple, 15-step, practical approach that equips anyone to work with children to help them become the experts.

Kids' Skills is a salutary reminder that children can find ways to overcome their difficulties; when we help them discover strengths and abilities that their problems had previously hidden from them. It is both that simple—and that complex.

Oh, and be warned—it involves having fun!

Michael Durrant
Director, Brief Therapy Institute of Sydney
Senior Clinical Associate, School of Psychology, University of Western Sydney

Contents

'Seriously Optimistic'
Publisher's Preface

Innovative Resources is the publishing arm of St Luke's Anglicare, one of Australia's leading community service organisations. Our favourite term for describing ourselves is 'seriously optimistic'. As publishers in a world so often dominated by stories of doom and gloom, we produce materials for human service workers that attempt to challenge the pervasive cultures of fatalism and loss of hope. We are optimists and we are serious about it!

It is this same sense of serious optimism that we saw in Ben Furman's work over a decade and a half ago. It is a long way between Australia and Finland but we have retained an ongoing admiration for Ben's approach to therapy. Indeed, I believe we have developed a mutual kinship and passion for pushing the boundaries of strengths-based practice.

We felt honoured when Ben offered us the opportunity of publishing an English version of Kids' Skills because of its neat fit with the four criteria we attempt to adopt in all our 'seriously optimistic' publications:

1. Kids' Skills is practical and immediately useable. It does not demand extensive prior training or theoretical understanding. It is creative yet clear and simple to incorporate into practice and celebrates the expertise of the client, not our own professional cleverness.

2. Kids' Skills is inspirational. It is a set of ideas that build creativity by suggesting new possibilities. You can choose to use the whole model or any of its parts by themselves. Or you can use the underlying ideas to create your own metaphors and activities.

3. Kids' Skills has a gentle, playful humour. Humour can be a powerful catalyst for change and in Kids' Skills the humour is subtle and understated, but present none-the-less. In the world of 'therapeutic' literature, which can be highly pretentious, this playful humour acts to help make sure that we don't take ourselves too seriously.

4. Kids' Skills is political. It may not read as polemic for social action but Kids' Skills does have a political agenda. Here in Australia, at the time of writing, we have children locked up in detention centres—read 'prisons'—simply because their parents wanted to give them a life of freedom and hope. We have children living with disabilities but still treated as second-class citizens and we have thousands of Indigenous children whose futures are being whittled away by violence, sexual abuse and the fumes of petrol and solvents. Kids' Skills represents an affirmation of the fundamentals of children's rights and makes many useful suggestions for ways to ensure our children are heard and treated respectfully.

So thanks, Ben, for your creativity and vision.

Thanks also to the team at Innovative Resources for bringing Ben's manuscript to fruition at such a high aesthetic standard.

To Alan Simpson, copyeditor *extraordinaire*, thanks for leaving no stone unturned. We know we handed you a huge challenge to fine-tune the cultural nuances of the text. Your diligence, as always, is remarkable. Readers will notice that Alan has tried to retain the authentic presence of Ben's original culture and language, while rendering the text in simple English. He has also ensured an even mix of gender pronouns ('he', 'she') throughout the book.

To Brad Welsh, thank you for your page design and layout. Your contribution has greatly enhanced the aesthetic appeal and readability of this book. Brad has used a different font for the many anecdotes contained in the book (also, the first few words of these stories are in bold) for readers who want to locate them at a glance.

To Brent Seamer, a big thank you for your cover design. To Brent's son, Tylar, thanks for letting us use your inspirational photo for the front cover image. (Tylar, remember: always trust your cape!)

Finally, to Karen Masman, our managing editor, thank goodness I have people like you around me who are thorough and systematic. Without Karen this wonderful English version of Kids' Skills would still be struggling to see the light of day.

To our many loyal supporters and hopefully, to the hoards who may discover us through Kids' Skills—enjoy and be inspired.

Russell Deal
Publishing Director

Ways to use this book

You can use this book in a number of ways, depending on what your interests or needs are. You can use it as:

A textbook for using the Kids' Skills method

You can think of this book as a textbook, the aim of which is to teach you to use the Kids' Skills method with your own children or the children you work with. In this case, read the book in the conventional way from cover to cover, discuss the contents with other people, and learn the method by putting it into practice.

An introduction to solution-focused education and therapy with children

You may also think of this book as a theoretical piece of literature, the aim of which is to familiarise you with the new and revolutionary psychological approach known as solution-focused psychology. In this case, read the book wearing your critical glasses and scrutinise the ideas with your friends or colleagues. Speculate on what implications the ideas presented in the book would have, if adopted by society at large. How would the ideas influence the way we raise and educate our children? What effect would they have on the way we guide families seeking help when their children experience problems?

A collection of good ideas for parenting and raising children

A third way to use this book is to think of it as a compilation of creative ideas and techniques which have been found useful in dealing with children. The Kids' Skills method consists of fifteen steps. You can conceive of these steps as a sequential program to be carried out from beginning to end, but you can also see them as a collection of independent ideas that you can use creatively in appropriate situations.

What is Kids' Skills?

All children, at some point during their years of growth, experience challenges. For some, these challenges lead to the development of issues such as anxiety, tantrums, difficulties in learning certain things. Usually such issues come and go, but sometimes they seem to become established – and then the adults caring for the child begin looking for solutions. This is the point where they need ideas.

Kids' Skills is one such idea. It is a method by which children overcome difficulties in a positive and constructive way by learning new skills.

Kids' Skills was originally developed in Finland, at the Keula preschool for children aged four to seven, but it was soon found that the approach fits older children as well. In fact the principles of Kids' Skills have little to do with age. With some modification the approach can be used in helping teenagers and even open-minded adults to work through most issues.

The Kids' Skills program comprises fifteen sequential steps. As you read the book you may find yourself wondering how strictly you should follow the program when working with children. You may wonder, for example, whether it is critical to include all of the steps in the process or whether you should complete the steps in the exact order in which they have been described.

When people take lessons in ballroom dancing they may ask their teacher whether it is better, when out on the dance floor, to improvise or to stay with the steps they have learned. A dance teacher would typically answer by advising the students to begin by following the steps exactly as taught, and to start improvising only when they feel secure and comfortable in the dance. In other words, when they become one with the rhythm of the dance. Only then should the dancer start to experiment by changing the order of the steps, leaving out some steps, or even adding new steps to the dance.

This principle applies to Kids' Skills as well. As soon as you become familiar with the steps and have a feel for Kids' Skills, you can begin to improvise in order to find your own personal way of applying the ideas – whether with your own children, or the children and families you work with. It is good to keep in mind that Kids' Skills is not intended to be yet another educational method telling you what to do and what not to do with your children. Rather, it is a raft that will help you cross the river to the other side, to a place where you can reclaim the creativity and fun that is so crucial in helping children meet their challenges.

Converting problems into skills

Dan was a boy of six with an inconvenient behaviour. He refused to use the toilet like everyone else and soiled his underwear instead. His parents had tried many things to help him, to no avail. Dan suffered as a result of this delay in his development; other kids often shunned him and he was rarely invited to play at friends' houses. Also, the possibility of attending a summer camp was out of the question.

However, the summer just before his seventh birthday, Dan started to go to the toilet regularly like everybody else. One day his mother brought up the issue with him.

'You don't know how happy I am now that you have finally learned to use the toilet regularly,' she said. 'Isn't it nice for you too?'

'Yes it is,' said Dan, and then he continued: 'It took me quite a while, but in the end I learned it!'

This story illustrates the basic idea of Kids' Skills. When children refuse to go to the toilet and soil their underwear, adults usually think this is a symptom of some serious underlying disturbance. But Dan saw it differently. His words – 'in the end I learned it' – show that for him, going to the toilet regularly was simply a skill that all children need to learn, the only difference being that it took him longer than other children.

Kids' Skills is based on the notion that children do not actually have problems, only skills they have not yet learned. In other words, most issues confronting children – including fears, bad habits, and disorders involving sleep, eating, urinating and defecating – can be perceived as undeveloped skills. By learning the relevant skills, children overcome the corresponding problems.

In Kids' Skills we start the problem-solving process by 'converting' problems into skills – that is, moving from the perception of a 'problem' to an awareness of the skill required to overcome it. This step is called 'skilling'. When we have identified the particular skill the child needs to learn for the problem to disappear, we can start to talk about skills rather than problems. After all, the thought of learning skills is far more appealing to children – and more motivating – than the thought of dealing with difficulties.

Building motivation

Coming to an agreement with a child about which particular skill needs to be acquired does not guarantee that the child will automatically become motivated to learn that skill. We may still have to do various things to build the child's motivation, to help her become truly interested. There are a number of things we can do to build the child's motivation. For example, allowing the child to come up with a name for the skill to be learned, helping the child see the advantages of learning this skill, and making plans with the child – well in advance – about how she can celebrate her acquisition of it. In addition, we can make sure that there are a number of people who are willing to support and help the child as she is learning.

Practising the skill

When we have succeeded in getting the child interested in learning the skill, we encourage him to start practising it. We also find suitable ways for the child to practise the skill, and make sure he gets lots of positive feedback whenever he practises and performs it.

Because learning rarely follows a straight line, we must also be prepared for setbacks – times when the child temporarily loses the skill and the problematic behaviour reoccurs.

Reinforcing learning

When the child has learned her skill, we arrange a celebration in her honour. Before the celebration we encourage the child to acknowledge all those people who supported or helped her. As another important part of the process, we try to arrange an opportunity for her to pass her newly learned skill on to someone else, and finally, with the child's input, we agree upon the next thing for her to learn.

The Birth of Kids' Skills

In the mid-1990s two creative special education teachers, Sirpa Birn and Tuija Terävä, contacted me to ask me to become their supervisor. These two women worked at the Keula preschool for children with special needs and were exceptionally enthusiastic about their work with children and families. I met with Sirpa and Tuija soon thereafter to discuss how I could best be of help to them. In this meeting we came up with the following idea: I would not be their supervisor in the conventional sense of the word (having regular meetings to discuss their cases) but we would work together to develop a method of resolving the problems that children face. This method could then be taught to anybody who needed ideas about how to help children deal with difficulties. This cooperation gradually led to the birth of what was later to be called Kids' Skills.

The goals

At the outset of the project we set ourselves a number of clear goals. First of all, we wanted to create a method that was effective and useful for working with many kinds of children's issues. The method was to lend itself to resolving those ordinary, everyday issues that any parents may encounter in raising their children, as well as those more serious problems that come to the attention of professionals specialising in helping children with significant needs.

The method was to be straightforward and easily understandable, as it was important for us that anybody caring for children could adopt it and benefit from using it. It was to be applicable to different environments such as homes, schools, preschools, child guidance centres, children's homes and so on.

We also wanted the method to be approved of by children. In my work with children over the years I have become convinced that for us to obtain results we need the child's full cooperation. With this in mind, it was important to us that our ideas worked on children's terms, and that children would find the method appealing.

But it was not enough for us that the method be well liked by children. We also wanted it to be appreciated by parents, and we wanted it to improve the relationships amongst all the adults caring for the child. This required that the method be based on a psychology that did not blame anybody for the issues involving the child but instead would view everyone as a resource. All those close to the child were to be seen as supporters, capable in one way or another of helping the child learn the skill he needed to learn.

With these goals in mind we began our work. We met every couple of weeks developing ideas that Sirpa and Tuija, together with their colleagues, tested at Keula preschool. My colleague Tapani Ahola also took an active role in developing the ideas. Gradually, through many a trial and error, we were able to describe a fifteen-step program which was given the name Kids' Skills.

Kids' Skills comes of age

Now that Kids' Skills has received wide acceptance not only in our own country but in quite a few other countries as well, we can safely say that it has met the goals we originally set for it. It works well, children love it, and parents without exception feel positive about it. It has a positive effect on the relationship of the child's parents, and it favours staff–parent cooperation when used in schools and other institutions. Above all, Kids' Skills is simple enough to be adopted by anyone, by parents and teachers as well as those who work professionally in the field of helping families cope with the issues their offspring face.

Kids' Skills requires a new way of thinking

Kids' Skills is a simple method, but applying it is not quite as easy as it might seem. Adopting the method requires us to take on a new way of thinking, and putting the method into practice takes effort.

Western psychology has taught us to think that problems experienced by children are usually caused by environmental factors, such as what their families are like or how their parents have raised them. As a result of this line of thinking, whenever children face problems parents tend to begin to blame each other. 'That's what you get from always giving in to him!' or 'No wonder she's like that. You're always pushing her!' or 'We've never had any of those problems on my side of the family!' This same phenomenon – 'blamestorming', as it is sometimes called – also manifests itself when children face issues at school. 'He'd do much better at school if you showed some interest in his homework,' a teacher may say when talking with a child's parents. The parents would typically experience the teacher's words as an accusation and would, in turn, respond accordingly: 'He was doing much better at school last year when he had another teacher!'

Kids' Skills prevents 'blamestorming'. When we use it, we do not devote much time to finding out the original cause of the child's difficulty. Instead we focus on what the child needs to learn, thus avoiding those typical fault-finding conversations so characteristic of more traditional approaches to childhood issues.

Having said that, I would like to point out that this does not mean we close our eyes and deny the fact that there may also be negative influences in the child's environment. On the contrary. In Kids' Skills we focus on helping children learn skills, but at the same time the approach has positive effects on the environment in which the child is growing. Kids' Skills helps people pull in the same direction, it directs adults as well as other children to become more supportive of the child, and it offers everyone a chance to feel important and useful by helping the child learn her skill.

Kids' Skills forces us to re-examine the way we cooperate with children. Traditionally, children have been regarded as targets of parenting, education and therapy. This is not to say that children have never been allowed to participate in any discussions concerning them. They have. The point is that children have been given little opportunity to talk about how their issues are resolved. In Kids' Skills this is different. Here children are not seen as targets of adult intervention, but as rightful partners who are expected to participate actively in all decisions concerning them.

Parents often feel embarrassed to admit their children are struggling. When they talk about the issues with teachers at school or with professional helpers, they usually do so behind closed doors. In contrast, Kids' Skills is characterised by openness. Once the problem has been converted into a skill to be learned, it is possible to talk openly about the skill and the learning. The benefit of this openness is that everyone, adults as well as the child's friends, can participate together in supporting the child while he is learning the skill.

In the Western world we have been trained to think that when a child is struggling we should turn to experts who then examine the child and recommend a treatment provided by professionals. Experts will always be needed, but Kids' Skills looks for another course of action. It strives to pass on the know-how of resolving childhood issues to those who most need it – the parents, teachers, nurses, and all the other people who work in the frontline of caring for children and helping families. Adopting Kids' Skills challenges the routine of relying on experts, while requiring us to accept the idea that the best keys to a solution may actually lie in our own hands.

The 15 Steps

Step 1 Converting problems into skills

Find out what skill the child needs to
acquire to overcome the problem.

Step 2 Agreeing on the skill to learn

Discuss the issue with the child and
agree on what skill he will start learning.

Step 3 Exploring the benefits of the skill

Help the child become aware of the advantages
of having the skill.

Step 4 Naming the skill

Let the child give the skill a name.

Step 5 Choosing a power creature

Let the child choose an animal, or some other
character, to help her learn the skill.

Step 6 Gathering supporters

Let the child invite a number of people to
become his supporters.

Step 7 Building confidence

Help the child build confidence in
her ability to learn the skill.

Step 8 Planning the celebration

Plan with the child, ahead of time, how to
celebrate when the skill has been acquired.

Step ⑨ Defining the skill

Ask the child to tell you, and to act out for you,
how she will behave when she has acquired the skill.

Step ⑩ Going public

Inform people what skill the child is learning.

Step ⑪ Practising the skill

Agree with the child about how she
will practise the skill.

Step ⑫ Creating reminders

Let the child tell you how he wants
others to react if he forgets his skill.

Step ⑬ Celebrating success

When the child has acquired the skill, it is time
to celebrate and to give her an opportunity to
acknowledge all those who helped her learn it.

Step ⑭ Passing the skill on to others

Encourage the child to teach the new skill
to another child.

Step ⑮ Moving on to the next skill

Find agreement with the child about
the next skill to learn.

Converting problems into skills

Find out what skill the child needs to acquire to overcome the problem

For every developmental issue there's a skill to learn

Kids' Skills is based on the idea that issues confronting a child are best resolved by having the child learn a specific skill. This idea is based on the observation that when a child is faced with a problem, it is often due to the fact that there is some skill lacking, and that when the skill is acquired the problem goes away.

At first this may seem like splitting hairs. But the switch to talking about skills instead of problems is not an attempt to be smart. Once we begin talking about skills instead of problems we find that it becomes far easier – for children as well as adults – to discuss matters in a constructive way.

Let's imagine that you are the mother of a wild boy. His teacher comes to you and says, 'Your son behaves aggressively towards the other children in the class.' How do you react to her words? Do you thank the teacher for bringing the issue to your attention and begin to discuss it with her calmly? I doubt it, because that would make you an exceptional parent.

If you are a normal parent, you feel that you have been blamed and you react accordingly by doing what people do when they feel attacked. You defend yourself by deflecting the blame onto someone else. You might say, for example, 'He never does that at home' or 'That's because he is being bullied by his classmates' or even 'I am never aggressive so he must have got this behaviour from his father!'

On the other hand, how would you react if the teacher brought the same issue up in a different way? She wouldn't say a word about your son's problematic behaviour but would approach the issue by talking to you about the skill she thinks your son needs to learn. Here's what she might say:

I've spoken with my colleagues about Karl, and we've been thinking about the most important thing for him to learn so that he can be successful at school. We've come to the conclusion that it would be important for him to develop better self-control and to stay cool even when others are not kind to him. How do you feel about this idea?

Disarming, isn't it? How would you react now? You might even consider saying something like, 'I have thought about the same thing' or 'He definitely needs to develop better self-control, and to tell you the truth, I would have a use for that ability myself.'

Talking about skills to be learned rather than problems to be overcome is a more constructive and cooperative way of approaching the issues that children face.

Skilling – finding the skill behind the problem

When we begin to view problems as skills to be learned, we soon learn to see what skill a child needs to learn (or become better at) to resolve a particular issue. Say a child is impatient and wants everything to happen at once. We would most likely say that she needs to develop her ability to wait. We have found the correct skill if we can predict that acquiring that skill will do away with the problem.

However, seeing problems as skills to be learned is not necessarily simple. Converting problems into skills, or 'skilling', is a skill in and of itself, a skill we all can learn and develop further. Many people who have learned Kids' Skills have found this step to be the most difficult.

When we get down to 'skilling' a problem, we might benefit from asking the question: *What does the child need to learn for the problem to disappear?*

Let's imagine, just for the sake of testing the above question, that you have a child with the socially inappropriate habit of picking her nose. You might answer the question by deciding that the child needs to learn to clean her nose with a handkerchief (rather than doing it with her finger).

When thinking about the skill that takes care of the problem, we should always keep in mind the rule of solution-focused psychology, according to which *a skill should never involve stopping doing the wrong thing but learning to do the right thing instead.* The following examples illustrate this rule:

- If a child wets his bed at night, the skill for him to learn is not to stop wetting the bed but to wake up to go to the toilet during the night, or to acquire the ability to wait until the morning.

- If a child plays with food, the skill for her to learn is not to stop playing with food but to eat properly.

- If a child dawdles when putting on his clothes, the skill he needs to learn is not to stop dawdling but to put his clothes on swiftly.

When the child has many issues

'But our child does not have only one issue, she has loads of them!' This is what some parents say when they think about how to help their children overcome difficulties with Kids' Skills. You will find that it is easier to help children deal with issues if you replace the idea that they have many problems with the idea that they simply have several skills to learn, or to improve upon.

When we have succeeded in converting all the issues into corresponding skills, the original list of 'problems' has turned into a list of skills to be learned. Few children are capable of learning several skills at once, and therefore the next thing to do is to decide, preferably with the child, which of the skills the child should learn first.

In such a case it may be wise not to start with the most difficult skill on the list, but with one of the easiest instead – even if it is just learning to say 'thank you' after a meal. This way we can increase the likelihood that the child will succeed in learning the skill, which will boost his confidence and prepare him for learning the next skill, even it is considerably more difficult.

I spoke about eight-year-old Mike with his teacher and his mother. Mike was not with us at the time. His mother and his teacher told me that Mike had many issues. Among other things he dawdled in the mornings so that he was frequently late to school, he didn't seem to find the energy to do his homework unless there was an adult to help him all the way through it, and he flew into tantrums at the smallest of setbacks. It did not take long for us to come up with a list of skills Mike needed to learn.

Mike's mother looked at the list and asked, 'OK, so which one of these skills should Mike begin learning first?' I was unsure, so I asked for the opinion of both mother and teacher. After thinking about it for a while they came to the conclusion that the most important thing for Mike to learn right then was to arrive at school on time. That was a good skill to start with. It was not too difficult for Mike to learn, and success in learning that skill would probably pave the way for Mike to learn the other skills as well.

Splitting complex problems into parts

Converting a 'big', or complex, issue into a single skill can be difficult. Common examples of complex issues include poor concentration, weak ego, low self-esteem, and lack of empathy. We can make 'skilling' such big issues easier by starting with splitting them into parts and then converting those parts into corresponding skills one by one.

I was teaching a workshop on resolving childhood issues when one of the participants, a special education teacher, told us about an extremely timid boy in her class who, in her words, had practically no self-esteem at all.

One day the teacher had asked all the children in the class to draw a picture representing themselves. This particular boy had drawn a picture of a tiger. This was surprising because the boy resembled a frightened mouse much more than a tiger.

A discussion ensued about why this timid boy had drawn a picture of a tiger to represent himself when this image was so far from the truth. The teacher speculated that this was the boy's way of saying what he wasn't, but what he wished he was. We played with this idea for a while and came to the conclusion that perhaps he wanted to say that there was a tiger lurking inside him just waiting to be unleashed.

The idea of the inner tiger triggered some laughter at first, but after a while the image started to become alive in our minds. It allowed us to divert our attention away from the many problems the boy faced to the abilities and qualities he needed to discover in himself to develop in the desired direction. The metaphor of the tiger helped us catch sight of skills and competencies he needed to acquire, such as 'daring to answer the teacher's questions in class', 'allowing the teacher to hang his drawings on the classroom wall', and 'daring to join the other children in play'. It is often difficult to address directly such 'big' problems as low self-esteem, but once we split the big thing into a number of small skills to be learned, we immediately start to get ideas about how the child might learn those skills – in order to awaken the tiger within.

Poor concentration is another example of a complex problem that is far easier to work with once we split it into smaller parts. After all, when we think about it, 'lack of concentration' is not really a problem as such. It is an umbrella term for a broad range of more specific problems. If we list all of these, and convert them into corresponding skills, we might end up with a list like this:

- To be able to stay in one place for a certain period of time
- To be able to listen to people without interrupting them
- To be able to wait one's turn
- To be able to raise one's hand when needing to say something in class.

To be able to play with other children is yet another example of a big skill that would be hard to 'crack' without first splitting it into a number of smaller skills.

Harry's quick temper in preschool was so bad that he was not allowed to play with other children without constant supervision by the staff. When Harry was asked what skill he wanted to learn, he said he wanted to learn to play with other children. Harry knew that to do this he needed to overcome his quick temper.

Harry's quick temper showed in many ways in the daily life of the preschool. One of the most alarming expressions of his temper was that when he was playing on the climbing frame in the playground he could suddenly become angry for no obvious reason and then shove another child off the frame onto the ground. The skill Harry most urgently needed to learn was to play with other children on the climbing frame without shoving anybody off. This was a simple and concrete enough skill for Harry to begin to practise right away.

For safety reasons, Harry started to practise his skill inside the school building. Once a week he was given an opportunity to climb up onto the bars in the school gym together with another child. When both of the children were up on the bars, Harry was to show the teacher and his classmates that he was able to play amicably with the other child for a while. When Harry had repeatedly demonstrated that he was able to do it, he was allowed to try to do the same on the climbing frame in the yard. He made rapid progress and within a month the staff felt they could safely allow him to play without constant supervision. What this meant in practice was that from then on Harry was allowed to go out to the playground even when the supervising teacher was still inside.

A skill is not stopping something

Let me emphasise that a skill is not an ability to *not do the wrong thing* but an ability to *do the right thing*. This is a simple principle but it takes some practice to get it right. When you ask people what skill they think a child should learn, it is very common to get a 'she-should-learn-not-to-do-that' kind of an answer.

The following four examples show how to move from what the child should *not* do to what the child *should* do instead:

'What skill should Sven learn?'

'He should learn not to be nasty to other children.'

'Right. So what is the skill he needs to become better at so that he's not nasty to other children?'

'He should learn to understand that he can't always be the one to tell everyone else what to do and what not to do.'

'All right, but in order not to do that, what is the skill he needs to learn?'

'He needs to learn to negotiate with others.'

'Sounds good. I am sure that Sven would understand there are benefits in learning to negotiate with others. Besides, learning that skill could be a lot of fun for him.'

'What skill should Sheena learn?'

'She has the bad habit of mimicking people. She should learn to stop doing that.'

'What does she need to learn to drop that habit?'

'She simply has to stop doing it, that's all.'

'That's correct, but let's remember that it's very difficult for children to drop bad habits if they don't have another habit to replace the bad habit with. So, what could this better habit be?'

'That I don't know, but I guess it's not so much a question of stopping mimicking as it is a question of learning to understand that sometimes it is OK to mimic people but at other times it's disrespectful and even hurtful.'

'So it's not that she should drop the habit of mimicking altogether, but that she should learn to tell when to do it and when not to do it?'

'Exactly. She should probably learn to ask people for permission if she feels like mimicking them, and at any rate she should learn to apologise if she hurts someone's feelings by doing it.'

'What skill should Mat learn?'

'He should learn not to lie.'

'He probably knows that he's not supposed to tell stories, but what does he need to learn so that he doesn't do that?'

'He just needs to stop telling stories.'

'But you don't want Mat to stop telling stories altogether, do you? After all, it is a skill to be able to make up exciting stories. Who knows, perhaps he will be a writer when he grows up.'

'No, I don't mean that he should stop telling stories altogether, but that he should learn to distinguish fact from fiction.'

'I guess that's an important skill for children to learn. Can we say that the skill Mat needs to learn is to be able to distinguish fact from fiction and to be able to tell people which one is which?'

'That's exactly the skill Mat needs to learn, because it's not that there is anything wrong with his stories. It's only that he doesn't understand that it's his duty to make it clear to people whether what he is telling is true or not.'

Teacher to pupils: 'What do you need to learn so that you are able to go to the school dining hall in an orderly way?'

'We need to learn not to run when we go there.'

'That's right, but what do you need to do instead of running?'

'We need to walk to the dining hall.'

'Very good. This is a skill you can practise. Let me write it down. And what else do you need to be able to do so that you can go to the dining hall smoothly?'

'We need to learn not to shove one another.'

'And what do you need to learn in order not to do that?'

'We need to learn to wait in line.'

'Good. I'll write that down too. That's also a skill you can practise.'

Don't's to Do's

You may have made the observation that when you ask your child to stop doing something you don't want her to do, your words may have no effect whatsoever. You say 'Stop that' and your child only continues as if you hadn't said anything.

'Don't shout!'
'Stop throwing things!'
'Cut out the kicking!'
'Don't play with your food!'
'Stop teasing your sister!'

In addition to the fact that these 'stop orders' often have little or no effect, they may in some cases actually provoke children to deliberately continue to do more of what they are doing. The good news is that children respond better to our orders when we express ourselves by telling them what we want them to do rather than what we don't want them to do. If we tell a child what we want to see him doing – and not what we don't want to see him doing – he won't feel criticised and therefore does not have a need to defend himself. I call the act of converting a don't-do-that statement into a do-this-instead statement 'don't to do'. Here are a few examples:

'Don't yell at me!'	→	'Talk softly.'
'No throwing things!'	→	'Keep those things to yourself.'
'Stop kicking!'	→	'Keep your feet still.'
'Don't play with your food!'	→	'Eat nicely.'
'Don't tease your baby sister!'	→	'Be kind to your baby sister.'

★ ★ ★

Kids' Skills starts with adults carrying out a conversation, usually in the absence of the child, about what skill they think the child should learn, or improve upon, to become free of a problem. When adults have come to an understanding of what skill they think the child needs to learn, they approach the child and propose that she learn that skill. In the next section we will talk about how to present such proposals to children and how to talk with them about skills they should learn.

Agreeing on the skill to learn

Discuss the issue with the child and agree on what skill he will start learning

There's nothing wrong with our children – it's just that sometimes they need to improve a skill or two

Jack was ten years old and his problematic behaviour was lying. He was seen, together with his parents and his teacher, by Andrew Duggan, a British therapist who uses Kids' Skills in his work with children. When Andrew had become acquainted with all those present in the session and had developed an understanding of the issue, he turned to Jack and said:

'Your father and your mother and your teacher seem to think that it would be good for you to learn to speak the truth instead of lying. Do you agree? Do you think it would be good for you to learn not to lie but to tell the truth instead?'

'Yes, it would,' said Jack.

'Are you sure? Do you really want to learn to speak the truth?'

'Yes, I'm sure,' said Jack, nodding.

Jack's willingness to learn the skill his parents and his teacher wanted him to learn is not unique. Most children readily agree to learn skills the adults caring for them wish them to learn. When we don't scold children for their unwanted behaviour but negotiate with them about the behaviour we want them to learn, they usually respond positively.

Here are some examples:

'You know, Jess, wouldn't it be good if you learned to be a bit more patient, so that you would be able to wait until your turn is up?'

'I have talked about you with Dad and we would like you to learn to be kinder to your sister. We know it's not easy, but once you learn to do that, I think we will all have much more fun, you too. How about if you start learning to be nicer to her? Would you like to learn how to do that?'

'All children in this class have skills they can become better at. I have thought about you, Zoe, and I think the skill that you might want to become better at is timing. You could learn to be in the classroom when the lesson starts. What do you say, Zoe? Would it be good for you to learn that skill?'

Proposing a skill to a child in a respectful manner makes it easier for children to say yes. This is not to say that children never turn down adults' proposals to learn skills. It does happen from time to time, no matter how respectfully we phrase our requests. Here are some ideas for how to make it even easier for children to respond positively to the proposal of learning particular skills:

Hint 1. Practise Kids' Skills with a group of children

When we first started to practise Kids' Skills in the Keula preschool for children with special needs, we agreed that all children in the group should have a skill to learn. The fact that all children (and not only those with particular issues) were learning a skill meant nobody was labelled as being different or abnormal.

When using Kids' Skills with groups of children, including families with more than one child, it is best to involve all the children. Perhaps not every child in the group or family will have an issue, but all children can work on some skill they need to improve. It is easier for a child to accept the idea that he needs to learn a skill when all the other children in the group or the family are also learning skills.

Hint 2. Use 'we' instead of 'I' when proposing the skill

Children find it easier to accept a proposal or a request to learn something when the proposal comes from several people rather than just one person. They respond more positively when we say, 'We want you to learn…' rather than, 'I want you to learn…'

Here are some examples of proposals using 'we':

'**I talked yesterday** with your father on the phone and we both agreed that you should learn how to take defeat when playing games. You'll enjoy playing cards and other games much more if you learn how to take it when you lose a game.'

'**I spoke with your parents** yesterday and they, too, feel that it would be important for you to learn to eat the same food the other children are eating. I know it's not easy but I'm sure you will learn once you start practising that skill with us.'

'**You have probably** already heard from your parents that we had a meeting here at school and that we came to the conclusion that the skill you need to learn is to be calmer in the classroom.'

Children value the fact that adults sit and talk about them, discussing what skills they need to learn. They know that to succeed in life, and to get along with their peers, they need many skills. Children tend to trust adults to have their best interests in mind when adults think about what skills they need to develop.

Hint 3. Negotiate with the child

When we talk to smaller children we may simply tell them outright that we want them to learn this or that skill. However, the bigger the child, the more important it is to negotiate with her about the skill to learn. We might be surprised at how aware children are about what skills they need to develop.

'**What skill do** you want to learn, Andrew?'

'I want to learn to drive a train.'

'Wow, that's a great skill to learn. I bet you can learn to do that when you grow up, but what skill do you want to learn now? What do you need to become better at so you can enjoy being here at the preschool?'

'I want to learn to play with the other children.'

'That's a wonderful suggestion. If you learn to play with the other children and you don't get into fights with them, I'm sure you'll enjoy coming here more. Do you think so, too?'

If you propose a skill for the child to learn and he refuses the offer, ask him what skill he would prefer to learn instead. Perhaps his own suggestion is better.

'**OK, Jasmine, if** you are not all that excited about developing your courage to speak up when you disagree with your friends' suggestions, what do *you* propose? What skill would you like to learn instead?'

'I would like to develop my courage to make my own suggestions.'

'Good thinking, Jasmine. If you have the courage to make your own suggestions you don't need to refuse the suggestions of others. You can simply suggest something else instead.'

Hint 4. Let children help each other to find the skills they need to learn

In multi-children families, schools and other institutions, the children usually know each other quite well and they can often tell what skills the other children in the group need to learn or improve.

A teacher used Kids' Skills with a class consisting of twenty-eight pupils. He started the project by informing all the parents about Kids' Skills. He did this to have the parents' approval for the project, but also to get them to become supporters for the children while they were learning their skills. The next step in the process was to find a skill for each child to learn. The teacher realised that it would take a long time for him to negotiate a skill for each child to learn individually. Instead he decided to put them into groups of four and ask the groups to find a skill for each group member to develop.

To help the children understand what kind of skills they were supposed to learn, he engaged the whole class in a general conversation about skills. During this conversation he drew a map on the blackboard depicting four 'skills' countries.

The first skills country was called the *School Skills Country.* The skills of this country were skills that children needed to succeed in school, such as taking care of their homework, raising their hands when they wanted to speak in class, and generally behaving well in the classroom.

The second skills country was called the *Friend Skills Country.* The skills of this country were skills that children needed to get along well with their friends, such as the ability to play with other children, the skill of intervening when a child was bullying another, and the skill of helping friends with homework.

The third skills country was called the *Adults Skills Country.* The skills of this country were various skills children needed in interacting with teachers and adults. Skills of this country included, for example, the ability to greet adults in a respectful manner, the ability to listen to adults, and the ability to talk with adults without using foul language.

The fourth skills country was called the *Courage Country.* The skills of this country consisted of various forms of courage that children needed to avoid being shy and fearful – such as the courage to speak up, the courage to refuse to do things that are forbidden, the courage to give an oral presentation, and the courage not to be ashamed if they happened to be different from other children in any way.

Once the children had participated in this discussion they had developed an understanding of what kinds of skills they were supposed to learn with the help of Kids' Skills. Now it was easy for them to help one another find their relevant skills.

Even if we come to an agreement with the child about what skill she is to start learning, it does not mean that the child is automatically motivated to learn that skill. Learning skills requires effort and therefore it is our next task to make sure the child is genuinely motivated and enthusiastic about learning the skill. The next few steps of Kids' Skills are dedicated to strengthening the child's motivation. The first one of these steps is to help the child to see what the many benefits of learning the skill are, not only for herself but for other people as well.

Exploring the benefits of the skill

Help the child become aware of the advantages of having the skill

The more benefits the child sees in learning something, the stronger her motivation will be

Motivation – what is it made of?

Where does the will to learn something come from? Why can children be highly motivated to learn one difficult skill and absolutely uninterested in learning another? The will to learn skills depends on many things. Above all, it seems to be linked to whether the child thinks that learning the skill has benefits or not.

It is not easy to learn to ride a bicycle, but children do not lack motivation when they come to learning that skill. Their eagerness is largely based on the fact that they can see there are benefits in learning to ride a bike. It's fun, it's a signal that you are a big girl or boy, and above all, it makes it possible for you to do fun things that would otherwise not be possible. We don't have to explain to children that it's a good idea to learn to ride a bike. It is obvious to them that being able to do so has many benefits.

Children are, however, not always aware of what the benefits of a particular skill might be. In fact, one reason why children don't always want to learn the skills that adults want them to learn may simply be that they are unable to see any benefits in learning that skill – for themselves, or for anybody else.

My younger daughter was eight when one day I suggested to her that she should learn to go to bed in the dark, or in dim light. This was because she had the peculiar habit of shining her bedside lamp directly into her face when going to sleep. I suggested that she learn to go to bed with the bedside lamp off and that we would let some light into her room through the door instead. She was far from enthusiastic about following my suggestion. I understood that her lack of enthusiasm stemmed from the simple fact that she couldn't see any benefits in learning that skill, not for herself or anybody else.

'What good will it do to learn to go to bed without the light on?' I asked her.

'Nothing,' she said.

'Come on,' I protested. 'It would do a lot of good.'

'What, then?' she asked in disbelief.

'First of all, if you were able to go to bed without the light on, I wouldn't have to go to your room to switch the light off every evening before I go to bed myself. And above all, I wouldn't have to go to bed wondering whether I had already turned your light off or not. That would save me from getting up from my bed and going to your room to check whether the light is still on or not.'

My daughter nodded, an understanding look on her face. We had uncovered the first benefit of learning the skill. As we continued the conversation about benefits we soon discovered quite a few more, and not only benefits for me but for her as well. For example, she came to realise that if she learned to go to sleep in dim light, she might receive more invitations from her friends to sleep over at their places. After all, most of her friends were used to going to bed in dim light and some were apparently disturbed by her need to have a bright light on. In addition, it would be easier to invite such friends to sleep over with her. I even brought up the fact that we would save quite a few cents on our electricity bill by switching off the light.

Having discussed for some time the benefits of learning to go to sleep in dim light, my daughter all of a sudden reached for the switch of the lamp and turned if off. Since that day she has never needed to have the bedside lamp on when going to sleep.

Discussions with children about the benefits of skills can lead to thoughtful conversations. Let's take the example of thanking adults for a meal. You say to your child that you want her to say 'thank you' when she finishes a meal. She asks you why you want her to do that. What is your answer? Do you say to her, 'Because I say so', or do you have a serious conversation with her about the benefits of saying 'thank you' after finishing a meal?

I was conducting a Kids' Skills workshop when this question was raised by one of the participants. 'What should I say to my child when he asks me why he has to say "thank you" after a meal?' We took her child's question seriously and searched for answers, working in small groups. When I collected all the answers we found that the participants had pulled out an impressive list of such benefits. The child's question turned out to be a useful question, definitely worth giving some serious thought.

What does 'benefits' mean?

A first grade teacher asked her pupils what benefits they would have from creating a good working spirit in the class. The pupils were able to say that they would enjoy school more but that was about all they could come up with. To help her pupils understand the idea of looking at the benefits of improving the class spirit, the teacher changed the subject and began to talk about reading and writing. She asked the pupils to tell her the benefits of being able to read and write. The children were able to answer this question; in just a few minutes there was a long list of the benefits of reading and writing on the blackboard. When the teacher then switched back to the topic of the benefits of a good working spirit, she found the pupils were able to produce an impressive list of benefits.

The meaning of the word 'benefits' may be self-evident to adults but children may find it difficult to understand. Therefore you may want to make sure the child understands what it means before you engage him in a discussion about the benefits of a skill:

'Would it be advantageous for you to learn this skill?'
'I don't know. It depends on what advantageous means.'

'It means, is it *useful* for you? Does it do you any good to learn it?'

'I guess so.'

'OK, so what do you think you will get out of it? What will you get out of having that skill?'

Everyone can contribute

It is not always easy for children to see what the benefits of learning a particular skill are. Fortunately other people, adults as well as their friends, can help them see the benefits of skills.

The parents of eight-year-old Peter wanted him to learn to sleep in his own bed because up until then the boy had been sharing their bedroom.

'Would it be good for you to learn to sleep in your own room?' the nurse asked Peter.

'I guess so,' Peter said. But judging by his tone of voice and his facial expression, he was far from excited about learning such a skill.

'What good will it do you?' the nurse continued.

'Nothing,' said Peter.

'But there must be some benefits in your learning to sleep in your own room. Otherwise I am sure your parents would not want you to learn it so much, would they?' The nurse was thinking aloud. She then turned to Peter's father and asked, 'What benefit will it bring you if Peter learns to sleep in his own room?'

'For me there would be many benefits because Peter sleeps rather restlessly and I frequently wake up during the night due to that. As a result I can be in a rather bad mood in the mornings and then I give everybody a hard time.'

'OK. What about you, mother? What good would it do you if Peter learned to sleep in his own room?'

'I used to think it was nice to have him sleeping in our bedroom,' the mother explained, 'but now I think he's too old for that. An eight-year-old boy should already be able to sleep in his own bed.'

'I hear you,' the nurse said, 'but can you tell me what good it will do you if Peter learns to sleep in his own bedroom?'

'What good…?' the mother thought to herself. 'Well, lots of good. First of all, when we go to bed at night, I would like to be able to have a chat with his dad about this and that, about children too. If Peter was sleeping in his own room, I could have a moment to speak about some adult things with his dad when we go to bed.'

The nurse turned to Peter. 'So now that we know what good it would do your parents for you to learn to sleep in your own room, I would like to know what good it will do you.'

Peter looked bewildered and didn't say anything. The nurse asked his parents to help him come up with an answer.

'Oh, I'm sure it would be good for you too,' his father said. 'It would be great for you to wake up in your own room in the morning and just start playing your games without having to wake us up.' Peter was listening attentively.

'And what about you, mother, what do you think it will do for Peter to learn to sleep in his own bed?' the nurse asked.

Looking at Peter, the mother said: 'I believe you'd sleep better and you'd be able to concentrate better at school. Who knows, maybe you'd even be able to get better marks! And think about it, you are already quite a handsome boy and in a couple of years girls will begin to get interested in you. When that happens, you wouldn't want to tell them that you still sleep in the same room with us, do you?'

The question of benefits to Peter if he slept in his own room was discussed in this way, with a twist of humour. The longer the list of benefits became, the more Peter himself became convinced that it was actually worth his while to learn to sleep in his own room.

What was true for Peter is true for other children too. For a child to become motivated to learn a skill, she needs to be convinced that learning it is worthwhile, that there are benefits for her, and others, in her having that skill. Everyone around her can help her to see what those benefits are.

For the child to learn the skill, he will have to start a project to practise it. For him to feel that the project is really his and not only something other people want him to do, it is a good idea to let the child give the skill a name. That is the topic of the next step of Kids' Skills.

Step 4

Naming the skill

Let the child give the skill a name

Your name, your game

Children are very creative with names. Anne Turner, an English school nurse who uses Kids' Skills in her work, says:

The names the children give their skills often surprise me. Some names are obvious, like 'hands off', whereas others are more subtle. One ten-year-old gave his listening-in-school skill the name 'football'. When asked why he'd called it this, he said that when you played football you had to listen to the coach and so he had to learn to do this in school as well. Another called his listening skill 'the dog skill' as dogs are very good at listening!

Anne also told me an example of what happens if a child takes his skill too literally:

There was a boy who needed to learn to sit still. He decided to call his sitting-still skill 'the chair skill'. The only problem with this skill was that the boy insisted on taking on a peculiar 'chair position' – with arms resting on invisible armrests. He stayed in this position for extended periods of time and wouldn't answer or speak to anybody while doing so. His behaviour was quite disturbing, but at the same time it was good practice for learning to sit still and be quiet. Fortunately, after a while he got the idea that he could put his hand up and speak in class when he needed to.

Children just love to name their skills. In one school, children named their skills according to various cartoon characters. One skill was called Pocahontas, another was called Lion King, and a third was called Mowgli, and so on. The creativity of children is boundless – what else can you say about such skill names as The Bear, Gentleman, Feet, The Princess School, Bananability, Simon-says ability, or Yes-skill?

Heroes lend their names to children

Children may be more creative in coming up with names for their skills than adults, but sometimes they still need help to spark off their creativity. One good way of inspiring children to come up with names for their skills is to help them think of particularly skilful heroes or heroines.

Eliza constantly interrupted other people. The skill she was to learn was the ability to listen to others. After a conversation about the benefits of the skill, she was convinced that it would actually pay off for her to learn it. But when her teacher asked her what name she wanted to give her skill, she said she didn't know. Nothing in particular came to mind, she said.

'Uh uh, it's not easy to come up with a good name for a skill like that,' the teacher sympathised with Eliza, and asked her to think about someone who was good at listening to others and who never interrupted when they spoke.

'Kitty is good at it. She never interrupts anybody,' Eliza said.

'Who's Kitty?'

'Kitty is our cat. She's an excellent listener.'

'Well, how about calling your skill "the Kitty skill"?' suggested the teacher.

Eliza immediately jumped at it. She thought it was a good idea and at that her skill was named.

If the child finds it difficult at this stage to come up with a name for the skill, don't worry. In the next step we will help the child find a power creature to help her learn the skill. Once we have done that, usually a name for the skill will spontaneously emerge.

Step 5

Choosing a power creature

Let the child choose an animal, or some other character, to help her learn the skill

A power creature helps the child reclaim his resources

I had just given a speech about Kids' Skills at an international conference on solution-focused psychology when a school psychologist came over to have a word with me. He said: 'What I like about Kids' Skills is that you allow children to use their imaginations in solving problems. I think it's a shame that imagination is so rarely used in the service of solving problems in this profession.' He related the following story to me:

I once met a boy who had this habit that whenever he walked past a light switch he simply had to go over to touch it. In the beginning it had simply been a harmless habit but soon it became worse. It was no longer enough for him to touch the switch once but he had to touch it exactly ten times. He suffered from this peculiar habit, and it didn't make it easier for him that the other children at school had started to make fun of him because of it. When I met the boy in my office I happened to ask him who did he think would be able to find a way out of a problem like this. He thought for a while and then said, 'Superman!' Superman, he explained, would have the power to find a way out of such difficult problems. At the end of our meeting I suggested to the boy that he try to act like Superman till our next session.

When I met him the next time in my office, two weeks later, he said that he had beaten his habit. I asked him to explain how he had done it. He said that he had simply started to act as Superman would have. I was puzzled, so I asked him how then would Superman have acted. He stood up, walked to the door and then came straight from the door towards me without touching the light switch. 'He would have done this. He would have just passed the light switch like this!' explained the boy proudly.

Children are inherently tenacious and resourceful beings and because of those qualities they can learn almost anything. To help them find their tenacity and resourcefulness, we ask them to pick a creature they like as their power creature – one that can help them learn the skills they need to learn. The power creature can be an animal, a cartoon character, or any other hero or heroine the child feels will give her the power to learn her skill.

The idea of humans having invisible beings helping them learn skills and overcome obstacles comes naturally to children. In fact, this idea is not only natural for children. Throughout the ages, in all cultures, people have drawn extra energy from benevolent spirits, guardian angels, saints, fairies, power animals and so on. For children the idea of power creatures comes naturally because, at some point in their development, many children have imaginary friends with whom they talk and play, and who help them in times of trouble.

Depicting the power creature

In Keula preschool there is a wall where all the children have their personal Kids' Skills posters. These small posters show the children's names and a description of the skill they are currently learning. In addition, the posters have a picture of the children's power creatures. In Keula it has been customary for the power creatures to be animals, so the posters have pictures of tigers, elephants, monkeys, dolphins, and so on. When new children start at the preschool, one of the first things that takes place is that they see the wall with the posters and the pictures of the animals. Usually the children then ask what the animals are, and when they learn that they are power animals they usually say, 'I want one too!' In fact, in Keula, Kids' Skills does not start with converting problems into skills but with children choosing their power animals. The children already have their power creatures when the discussion starts about what skills they should learn.

Children enjoy putting the picture of their power creature in a place where it can be seen. Sometimes they like to draw a picture of their power creature themselves, and sometimes an adult will draw the picture for them. The most common practice, however, is that children cut out pictures of their power creatures from magazines and other sources and then place the picture somewhere significant, such as on their Kids' Skills workbook or poster. These days you can also search the Internet and print out charming pictures of all kinds of power creatures.

How does the power creature help the child?

Power creatures can be helpful to children in many different ways. They can help remind children to practise their skills, and they can boost children's confidence in their ability to learn them.

In addition, power creatures can have other functions. They can act as consultants to children and offer advice to them, they can help them remember their skill if the unwanted behaviour returns, and they can share the child's feelings of success.

The power creature is a product of imagination and thus only fantasy sets limits to the ways in which it can be helpful to children in learning skills.

The power creature can

- help children become confident they will learn their skills

- give children strength to keep on practising until they learn their skills

- remind children when it's time to practise

- comfort and support children when they temporarily lose their skills

- help children recall times when they were able to perform their skills

- help children feel competent when they perform their skills.

Richard had developed the habit of spitting in his mother's face whenever he became angry. When he talked about this issue with his mother, he fully agreed that this was not the right thing to do. Yet the next time he got angry again he spat in her face as if they had never even discussed the matter. In the spirit of Kids' Skills, the mother suggested to Richard that he should learn to spit the words 'ush-ush' out of his mouth instead of spitting for real. Richard got the idea and dubbed the skill 'the ush-ush skill'.

His power animal was a big fat cat and he got to paste its picture onto a Kids' Skills poster, which was attached to the wall above his bed. Together his mother and Richard came up with a game for him to practise the 'ush-ush' skill. In this game, the mother would pretend to make him angry and he would then react by spitting the words 'ush-ush' from his mouth, instead of spitting saliva. Richard enjoyed the game and made rapid progress, with the result that he learned to spit the words 'ush-ush' out of his mouth not only in the game but also in real-life situations when he became genuinely angry.

However, the inevitable soon happened. One day Richard was angry with his mother again (for something not insignificant) and there was a setback. He forgot all about his skill and spat in her face as if there had never been any Kids' Skills training.

The mother did not panic, because she knew that setbacks are part of the package of learning new skills. Instead she said to him in a calm voice, 'Richard, now you have forgotten your skill. Your cat [Richard's power creature] must have thought that you'd already learned it. Perhaps he left to help other children learn similar skills. You might want to have a word with him to tell him that you still need him. Tell him that he shouldn't leave you until his job with you is over, when you master the "ush-ush" skill so well that you don't forget it any more.'

Richard, who had probably been afraid of his mother getting angry with him for spitting again, was baffled. He walked to his poster and had a serious talk with his cat. Later that day his mother asked Richard what he had said. He refused to tell her the details of the conversation but revealed that he had indeed asked the cat to come back and stay with him until he had fully learned to spit the words 'ush-ush' instead of actually spitting.

★ ★ ★

Children need the support of their power creatures, but they also need support from real people. The next step of Kids' Skills is devoted to gathering such 'live' supporters for the child.

Gathering supporters

Let the child invite a number
of people to become his supporters

The more supporters, the easier it is to succeed

For athletes to achieve victory they need sponsors and supporters to encourage and support them as they struggle to reach their goals. The same is true for children who are learning skills. They, too, need a good number of people to support them.

Supporters can be helpful to children in a variety of ways. They can, for example:

- encourage children by telling them they have made a good choice in deciding to learn that particular skill

- increase children's confidence in being able to learn their skills by telling them why they have faith in them

- admire children when they make progress and when they demonstrate their skills

- help children to get back on track when they temporarily forget or lose their skills

- share their joy whenever they succeed or make progress.

Supporters mean a lot to children. Children are more motivated to learn a skill when they know there are people who are keen to learn about their progress and who are anticipating that they will succeed. When we ask children which people they would like to ask to be their supporters, they often produce a long list of people.

Nine-year-old Toby was in trouble for telling lies. The skill he was supposed to learn was to speak the truth instead of telling 'porky pies', as he called his lying. ('Porky pies' is rhyming slang.)

'Who will you ask to be your supporters?' asked the family therapist at the child guidance centre.

'Could it be my friends?' asked Toby.

'By all means, but let's start with your family.'

'OK. Mum, Dad, my sister, Emma, and my cat, Stanley, because he calms me down.'

'Wow. I'll write all of their names in your workbook for you. Let's go on to school now. Who do you want to be your supporters at school?'

Toby mentioned the names of three teachers and said, 'Those are the three teachers I like the best.' Then he said, 'Can I go on to friends now?' and gave the names of five of his good friends, all of whom he was personally going to ask to become his supporters in learning to speak the truth.

Toby is not an exception. Children are usually proud of the skills they are learning and they like the idea of having several supporters. In addition, those who are invited by children to be their supporters are usually honoured by the confidence placed in them and are more than happy to accept the invitation.

Who can be a supporter?

Supporters are usually people who know the child well or have contact with her on a daily basis. The child's parents are usually her main supporters, but grandparents, aunts and uncles as well as any other close adults can be supporters for the child.

Adults are effective supporters but we have seen time and again that for many children, their peers (that is, friends, siblings, cousins and classmates) are even more effective. For this reason it is important, whenever possible, to make sure that the child's circle of supporters is not only comprised of adults but other children as well. If the child goes to a school where they have a mentoring system (that is, a system where older pupils support younger pupils) it is a good idea to include them in the circle of supporters. Other possible supporters include neighbours, sports coaches, as well as any therapists or health care professionals who might be working with the child.

The supporters need not always be members of the child's immediate social network. Family members in distant homelands – even when there is little or no contact at the time the child is learning the skill – can be important supporters. Sometimes children may even want to have a dead person included in their support circle. If the child has lost a loved one recently we might want to consider including that person too. For the child, having a lost loved one in his circle of supporters serves two purposes. On the one hand it allows the child to mourn the loss of that person, and on the other hand lost loved ones make good supporters. For children it is natural to imagine that, even if a person is dead, that person will still support them and rejoice in their progress.

'**Who do you want** to be your supporter when you try to learn the "princess" skill?' asked a mother.

'What's a supporter?' asked the little girl.

'A supporter is a person who wants you to learn the "princess" skill and who wants to help you learn it.'

'I want you and Dad to be my supporters.'

'All right. I will write "Mum" and "Dad" here [on the poster], where it says "supporters". Who else do you want to be your supporters?'

'Can I have Granny and Grandpa as my supporters?'

'Of course, dear, you can ask Granny to be your supporter. I am positive she wants to help you learn the "princess" skill. Grandpa is already in heaven but I am sure he would want to be your supporter, too. Let me write here "Granny" and "Grandpa". Do you want any other supporters? You like your godmother a lot, don't you? Shall we include her?'

Children don't think of death as something final, as adults do. Instead they usually think that dead people continue their existence in some other realm. For that reason it is natural for children to think that even if people are dead, it doesn't prevent them from acting as supporters for those who are alive.

If the child's parents are separated and one of them decides to use Kids' Skills to resolve an issue facing the child, it may be of crucial importance to involve the other parent as a supporter in the process. When the separated parents cooperate in helping their child learn a skill, they can sidestep the risk of blaming each other for the issue and become partners in supporting her.

The following example illustrates this point:

The separated parents of twelve-year-old Tina had the (not uncommon) habit of blaming each other for their daughter's behaviour. The mother decided to try to do something to change Tina's behaviour but she was afraid that whatever she agreed to do with Tina would be no use if Tina's father did not cooperate.

After having created a plan with Tina, the mother called the father and said: 'As you know, Tina has the bad habit of often yelling and talking back to me. We had a sincere conversation about this today and we came to an agreement that she would learn to talk to me in a respectful way. She named this ability "cooling", and said that she would want to ask you to be one of her supporters. How do you feel about that? Will you do it for her?'

The father was surprised, as he was used to Tina's mother blaming him rather than asking him to help her in working with Tina's issues. He said, 'OK, so how do you want me to support her?'

'You only need to say something that convinces her that you too think it's a good idea for her to learn the "cooling" skill. Also, you could show her that you're interested in her workbook. You know that Tina thinks highly of your opinion and I believe it would be very useful for her if you could be a supporter.'

Kids' Skills influences not only children but also all the adults who care for the child. One of its main strengths is its ability to generate cooperation among the adult carers.

How does the child ask someone to be a supporter?

Recruiting, or inviting people to become supporters, starts with the child deciding which people he wants to ask. When the list is complete, it is time to contact everyone to inform them that the child wants them to be in his support circle. This can be done in a number of ways. The best way is for the child to pass the invitation personally. People are usually delighted when children ask them such a thing. You can surely imagine how good it feels when a child you know comes and tells you that he is going to learn a particular skill, and then asks you: 'Do you want to be one of my supporters?'

Another, less direct, way for children to ask a person to be their supporter is for the child to present her Kids' Skills workbook or poster to that person and then to say, for example, 'If you want to be my supporter, you can put your name here. That's the page for the names of all my supporters.'

When Kids' Skills is used in schools, it is important that the children's parents participate as supporters in the process. A good way to involve the parents in their children's Kids' Skills projects is to give them the task of helping their children fill in their workbooks. When parents answer such questions as 'What are the benefits of learning the skill for the child, for the school, for the family?' or 'Why do you believe your child will succeed in learning the skill?' they automatically become their child's supporters.

Most of the time children ask people to become their supporters themselves. However, sometimes adults can do it for them.

'**Derrick has decided** to cut down on eating sweets and to stick to his "Sweet Saturday pack". It means he only has sweets on Saturdays. He would like you, Mike, to be one of his supporters. Would you like to do that? All you need to do is to praise him when he refuses sweets and then join the party we are going to have for him when he has succeeded in sticking to his "Sweet Saturday pack" for four weeks.'

★ ★ ★

Supporters can encourage and help children in many ways. They can show that they appreciate the child's decisions to learn particular skills, they can admire the child's power creatures, and they can help the child understand the benefits of learning his skills. While children are learning, their supporters can show interest in their progress, and when the skills have been acquired supporters can participate in celebrating the child's success. Supporters can be of help in all the steps of Kids' Skills – including the next step, which is dedicated to building children's confidence in their ability to learn their skills.

Building confidence

Help the child build confidence
in her ability to learn the skil

*When the child sees that other people are convinced he will be able
to learn his skill, he too becomes convinced that he can learn it*

Children are born optimistic. When we ask them, 'Do you think you will
learn this?' they usually answer in the affirmative regardless of what it is.
If we ask them why they are so convinced they can do it, they might say
something like, 'I just know I can.' This is often the case, but not always.

When children have trouble learning the skills that all their peers have
already mastered, they tend to become frustrated, discouraged and
demoralised. They start to think that there is something wrong with them
and that the skill is too difficult for them to learn.

In these situations children often say things like:

- 'I can't do it.'

- 'I'll never learn.'

- 'It won't work.'

- 'I'm no good!'

Children do not always express their demoralisation as openly as that. Sometimes they just lose interest in the task, or stop trying. The risk of demoralisation is, however, not restricted to children alone. Parents, in fact anybody caring for the child, can become frustrated and demoralised when the child has difficulty in learning skills he 'ought' to have – that is, skills most of his peers have already acquired. Adults sometimes express their demoralisation openly by saying things like:

- 'Come on, it's not that difficult!'

- 'Look at your baby sister. Even she can do it. How can it be so difficult for you?'

- 'Why can't you learn a simple thing like that?'

- 'This is a waste of time. You'll never get it!'

Such exclamations of disappointment may be understandable, but they do little to help children repair their fragile self-confidence.

A better way to boost children's confidence is to say something like: 'It may take a while for you to learn, but in the end you'll do it' or 'It's not that easy, but if you keep on trying, I'm sure you'll get it.'

When children notice that we appreciate the fact that it is not easy for them to learn certain skills, they can be easier on themselves. The bonus is that when their learning tasks are considered difficult rather than easy, children get a chance to feel proud of their accomplishments when they do make progress. After all, if we acquire an easy skill there's nothing much to be proud of. However, learning something that's considered difficult gives us ample reason to feel proud of our accomplishment.

How to build confidence

At Keula we have found a simple yet effective way to build a child's confidence in being able to learn new skills. We simply ask the child's parents and the other people who know her to tell her why they are convinced she will learn her skill.

'Your mum believes that you will learn to use the toilet just like all the other kids. It's not an easy skill for you to learn, but she's confident you can do it. She says that a week ago you sat on the toilet and succeeded. Let's ask your daddy what he thinks. Let's find out what makes him convinced that you'll learn.'

Dad: 'Of course I'm confident that you'll learn. Why wouldn't you? You're a stubborn lad. I've seen it when I'm playing football with you. And I can tell you from experience that stubborn lads learn whatever they want to learn!'

The point is that it's not enough to say to a child, 'I believe you'll learn' or 'You'll learn, there's no doubt about it'. We need to add a justification for our claim and to tell the child what it is we have noticed about him that makes us so convinced he will learn the skill. Otherwise there is the risk that the child thinks we are 'just saying it', even when we really do mean it.

Henry was a boy of twelve, for whom learning the multiplication tables was exceptionally difficult. All his classmates had already been able to memorise the tables but Henry had avoided the task because for him it seemed insurmountable. Henry's teacher had asked Henry and his parents to talk with her about the issue. When there was an agreement about the fact that Henry should learn the multiplication tables, the teacher asked him: 'Do you think you'll learn it?'

'I don't know,' said Henry.

The teacher started with his mother. 'What do you think, Mum? Do you believe he'll learn it?'

'There's no doubt about it in my mind,' Henry's mother answered.

'What makes you say that? Why are you so sure that he will learn?'

'Henry is good at learning things when he puts his mind to it. For example, he's the best in our household when it comes to using computers, so we know he really is a clever boy.'

Henry seemed pleased. The teacher then put the same question to his father.

'What about you, Dad? Do you also believe that Henry will learn the multiplication tables?'

'Of course he will if he decides to,' said his father.

'What makes you say that?'

'The multiplication tables were not that easy for me either at that age – and it may well be that Henry inherited this trait from me – but even I eventually learned, because my older brother didn't give up on me but taught me till I knew the tables inside out.'

'I guess it's my turn now,' said the teacher. 'I too believe that Henry will learn the multiplication tables soon, because recently he has made some remarkable progress. He has already mastered the two, three and five times tables, and if we don't count the one and ten times tables, there are only five more for him to learn.'

Judging by the look on his face, Henry had regained his confidence in his ability to learn the tables and to do what had seemed, up until then, impossible.

How to give good reasons for our confidence

We can justify our confidence in a child's ability to learn a skill in various ways. Here are some examples of common reasons people give when they justify their confidence to children:

- You have succeeded before.

- You have recently made progress.

- You have learned other difficult things before.

- You are so brave / determined / smart / quick, etc.

- You understand how important it is for you.

- You have so many wonderful supporters who will help you learn.

- It was difficult for so-and-so too, but she also learned eventually.

In addition to such rational justifications, children have no difficulty with more creative arguments, such as:

- 'I believe you will learn because you're a Sagittarian and Sagittarians have no problem learning these things!'
- 'I believe you will learn because you are almost as strong as Superman!'
- 'I'm sure you'll learn because you are like Pokemon!'
- 'I'm positive you'll learn because you have such wonderful parents!'
- 'I trust that you'll learn because I can see it in your eyes!'

Regardless of whether our arguments are rational or creative, the important thing is that the child hears a lot of people telling him why they are sure that he will learn his skill.

When we tell children our reasons for having faith in them, we help them regain their self-confidence by instilling them with ours. Allowing children to hear why we believe in them is an indispensable way to give them the 'spark' they need to learn their skills.

The only way a child can learn a skill is by practising or performing it over and over again. We will soon talk in detail about how children can practise their skills but before we do that, let's talk a little bit about how to celebrate when the child has acquired the skill.

Planning the celebration

Plan with the child, ahead of time, how to celebrate when the skill has been acquired

Planning ahead for the celebration sends the message to the child that he will be able to learn the skill

Children don't just love parties and celebrations. They also love planning and preparing for them. In Kids' Skills we engage children, early in the process, in planning for an event to celebrate learning their skills.

The anticipation of that event is a 'carrot' for children, boosting their motivation to learn. The planning of the celebration also helps build their confidence. Serious conversations about how to celebrate success at learning skills is a further indication to children that adults are confident they will succeed.

Linda was constantly in need of attention and was incapable of playing alone, even for brief periods. When Linda and her mother had come to an agreement that Linda would start learning the skill of playing alone at least for short spells, the mother asked Linda how she wanted to celebrate when she had learned to do it. Linda said she wanted to invite all her friends to a party where there would be balloons, streamers and cake.

Sam had fierce tantrums. The skill he was asked to learn was to be able to calm himself down when he was about to have a tantrum. He agreed with his parents that when he had learned the skill he would get to go out, together with both his parents, to see an ice hockey game.

Randy was learning the skill of making sure he had the right books with him for school every day. His parents agreed that when he had been able to perform this skill for two weeks in a row, they would take him and his younger brother to the park and would have a picnic there.

What does 'celebration' mean?

In Kids' Skills we use the word 'celebration' to refer to any kind of event arranged in honour of children who have acquired the skill they have been learning. A celebration is often similar to a birthday party, with cake and soft drinks, but it can also be a more modest event such as drinking juice and having snacks together around a table, or an outing to an interesting place.

At the time of the celebration children may also get symbolic rewards. For example, it was agreed with a boy who was a great fan of Michael Jordan that when he had learned his skill of 'guarding his tongue' he would get a cap from the Chicago Bulls, the team Michael Jordan played with. It is important to plan the celebration early on in the process because this way we can make sure that the anticipation of the celebration adds to children's motivation to follow through and to keep on trying until they have acquired their skills.

In some schools the number of children in a class is small enough to make it possible for the children to have their own personal celebrations. For example, at Keula preschool all the children get to have their own celebrations when they have learned their skills. The celebration is a ceremony, the details of which children can decide for themselves. The children may say, for example, which room the ceremony will be held in, what food or drinks will be served, and how the room will be decorated. Sometimes children want everyone to get dressed in a particular way, or to have face paintings. The essential thing about the ceremony is that it is personalised, and that the children have a say about the details. Not surprisingly, children at Keula are always anticipating their ceremonies with great enthusiasm.

Celebrating with large groups of children

When you use Kids' Skills in regular schools the number of children in a class may be so large that it is not possible to arrange separate ceremonies for each child. In these cases you could consider arranging a mutual ceremony for all of the children. The only 'but' is that all children may not have learned their skills at the time of the ceremony, but that need not be a problem if you think of the ceremony as a celebration of progress made, rather than skills having been fully acquired.

If you are a teacher and want to use Kids' Skills with your class, you may want to consider the following arrangement:

- Divide the pupils into 'mutual support teams' consisting of three to five children.

- Explain to the children that it is the duty of the teams to help each team member to find a good skill to learn and then to encourage and support each other to learn the skills.

- Have the pupils choose their power creatures and let them draw pictures of their creatures during art lessons.

- Ask the pupils to write their skill (in a few words) onto their drawings and let them hang these 'posters' on the classroom wall for everyone to see.

- Plan with the class, well ahead of time, how you will celebrate progress after an agreed time period – preferably a number of weeks. Remember to invite the parents to participate in the celebration.

When the child does not want a celebration

There are times when children do not want to celebrate learning their skills. This may be the case when children are so grown up that for them such celebrations appear too childish, or when there is an element of shame attached to not having learned the skill earlier. For example, if a twelve-year-old child learns to sleep in her own bed (rather than sleeping in her parents' bed), she may not want to make any fuss about her accomplishment.

Justin was ten years old. He had been wetting the bed and the skill he was learning was to be able to keep dry throughout the night. When Justin was asked how he wanted to celebrate after he had been able to do it for a fortnight, he said, 'I don't want to celebrate in any way.' He was very motivated to learn his skill but he disliked the idea of arranging an event that would only draw unnecessary attention to his situation.

Even older children like to celebrate

On the other hand, although the idea of having a celebration when a person learns a skill may appear childlike, experience has shown that some older children, and even adults, enjoy the idea that there will be some kind of ceremony to celebrate their accomplishment.

I am reminded of two seventeen-year-olds I once met at a teaching workshop. The two boys were studying at a technical college to become car mechanics and they had the same predicament: their number of days absent during the past term was so high that they had both received an ultimatum from the school. If they were absent any more they would not get their certificates at the end of the school year. The school counsellor had invited both boys together to our workshop to discuss their situation. As soon as I had learned that both boys sincerely wanted their certificates, I started to talk with them about the possibility of arranging a celebration if they reached their goals. When I asked them how they would celebrate if they succeeded, they had a word with each other and then said they would like to have coffee and cake together with their school counsellor in her office. Not a bad suggestion coming from two tough-looking adolescents lads.

Noah was fourteen years old, and had begun to steal. He had taken money from his stepfather, mother and grandmother – fortunately, not as yet from anyone outside the family. When we were thinking about what skill or ability Noah needed to develop to overcome his stealing, we came to the conclusion that he needed to learn to become trustworthy. The goal was, in other words, that all Noah's family members would be able to trust him again and that no one would need to worry about Noah going to their wallets without permission.

After we had an agreement with Noah that this was something he needed to learn, we started to talk about how the family might want to celebrate when Noah had regained his reputation as a trustworthy boy. The family came up with the plan that the following spring, at the end of the school year –

assuming of course that Noah had succeeded in convincing everyone that he had changed – there would be a small celebration at home where Noah would be pronounced trustworthy.

After some discussion back and forth it was decided that in addition to the immediate family, his grandmother and Noah's biological father (who was no longer living with them) would be invited to the celebration. I then asked them who would take care of telling Noah's grandmother and his biological father about this. The mother said she would do it. I complimented her on her helpfulness but suggested that it was perhaps better to let Noah take responsibility for speaking to his grandmother and his father about the upcoming celebration. After all, if he was responsible for stealing, he should also be responsible for doing whatever he needed to do to become an honest boy again.

It is worth planning how to celebrate success early on. However, the actual celebration will have to wait until the child has proved that he has acquired the skill. Before that, we need to generate a plan about how the child will practise it. But to be able to do that, we first need to develop a mutual understanding about what having that particular skill actually means in practice. That will be the topic of our next section.

Defining the skill

Ask the child to tell you, and to act out for you, how she will behave when she has acquired the skill

Show it today and tomorrow you can do it

Even when children say they need to learn a skill, they may not know what having that skill actually means in practice. Therefore it is important to talk to them about how they are supposed to act when they have acquired the skill they are learning.

- 'When you have learned to go to bed without fuss, how will you go to bed then?'

- 'When you no longer shove other children even if they tease you, then what will you do if someone teases you?'

- 'When you no longer play with your food and you eat properly, then how will you eat?'

- 'When you are able to say goodbye to your mother in the morning and you no longer cling to her, how will you do it?'

Show me how you will do it

It is useful to have a discussion with the child about how a person will behave once a given skill is acquired. This gives children ideas about what they are expected to learn. Asking children to act out or perform their skills allows them to develop an even better awareness of what having the skill really means in practice.

'OK, let's imagine that it's night-time. You are going to bed. You have learned to go to bed without a fuss and you are able to do it in the way you said you would. Now show me how you do it.'

'Let's suppose that another child comes to you and says something rude to you. You know exactly how to handle the situation in the way we talked about. What would happen? Say, here comes this rude child [holding a doll] and he starts to tease you. Show me what you do.'

'Let's pretend that you have learned to eat properly. Imagine that this is the dining table here and this is the food. Show me how you can eat properly.'

'Picture yourself one morning in the future when you have learned the skill of saying goodbye to your mother. Now, I'm your mother leaving to go to work. Show me what you do when I say goodbye to you.'

Simon found it difficult to go home with his dad after preschool in the afternoon. When his father came to pick him up he threw a tantrum, began to swear, and did everything he could to extend his stay at the preschool. The skill Simon agreed to learn was the skill of leaving the preschool with his dad 'like a gentleman'.

When Simon was asked to explain how he would leave the preschool with his dad once he had learned his skill, he said, 'When Dad comes to pick me up and says, "Let's go", I'll grab his hand and I'll say, "OK".' Simon was given a chance to demonstrate the skill right away. His father left the room and closed the door behind him. Next minute he returned, extended his arm towards Simon and said, 'Let's go, Simon!' Simon took his dad by the hand and said, 'OK, let's go!' The performance went well and then Simon was given an opportunity to replay the scene with his father.

However, this second time the task was made a little more difficult for Simon. He was to go and play with Lego with his friends – an activity he liked a lot – and then his father was to appear and interrupt his game and say, 'All right, Simon, time to go home!' Simon was to demonstrate that he was able to handle this more demanding situation. Simon stopped playing, grabbed his dad by the hand and said, 'OK, let's go!' His friends gave him spontaneous applause.

Six-year-old Minnie was afraid of dogs. The therapist at the child guidance clinic agreed with Minnie that to overcome her fear of dogs the skill she needed to learn was to like dogs and to enjoy their company.

The therapist then asked Minnie: 'What will you do when you meet a dog once you have already learned to like and enjoy them?'

'I won't run away.'

'I bet you won't. What will you do instead?'

'I'll go close to them and stroke them.'

'You won't go ahead and stroke all the dogs you see, will you?'

'Of course not. I will always ask the owners first if it's OK to stroke them.'

'That sounds really good to me. But suppose one day in the future, when you have already learned to like dogs and enjoy their company, you walk down the road and then suddenly, out of the blue, there comes a person walking a big dog? What will you do? Will you panic and cross the street, or stay calm?'

'Of course I won't panic if I have already learned to like dogs. I will stay calm and just walk past the dog calmly,' said Minnie.

The therapist talked with Minnie in this way for a while until both of them started to have a clear picture about what learning to be comfortable with dogs would mean in practice. The next step was to ask Minnie to act out the behaviour that had been discussed.

'Let's imagine now that this teddy bear is a dog and that I am its owner. You stand there and I will suddenly appear from around that corner with this dog. You can then ask me if the dog is nice or angry. Do you want to try?'

Minnie was eager to try the role-play. The therapist went around the corner with the teddy bear and when she appeared with it, Minnie immediately asked her if the dog was nice or angry. The therapist answered that the dog was nice, upon which Minnie went over to the dog to stroke it gently. The role-play also gave the therapist an opportunity to explain to Minnie how to approach dogs in the right way, and about the importance of always letting them smell you before you stroke them.

Let's give it a try

I met Will and his mother in my office.

'Things have been much better lately,' Will's mother explained.

'I'm glad to hear that,' I said, 'but are there still any issues left?'

'The only thing that's a bit of a problem is that Will doesn't do his homework unless I sit beside him all the time.'

'Do you mean that he needs help with his homework?'

'Not really,' said his mother. 'He can take care of the homework himself. It's just that I have to be next to him while he's doing it and I don't really have the time, particularly now that the baby needs so much attention.'

I turned to Will. 'It seems that your mum wants you to learn to do your homework on your own. Do you agree that this would be a good skill for you to learn?'

'Yes, it would,' answered Will with enthusiasm.

'What would it mean in practice? When you can do your homework on your own, where would you be doing it?'

'In my own room.'

'Wow! You'd be doing your homework in your room all by yourself. How long would you be working for without anybody standing or sitting next to you?'

'For an hour.'

'For an hour, all by yourself! That must be difficult if you are used to having someone sitting beside you all the time. Shall we make a test to see how that would work?'

Will was willing to give it a try so I took a piece of paper and scribbled down a few simple mathematical problems on it. I asked him to come with me to the next room, where I sat him at a table with a pen and paper and the problems.

'I'll go to talk with your mum for a while. You can come back to us when you are done so we will see how you'll manage doing homework all by yourself.'

I chatted with his mother for approximately ten minutes, then Will appeared. I looked at his answers and complimented him on the correct results. Even if this was just a game, it was at the same time a confirmation that Will was able to do homework on his own. In addition the exercise gave Will and his mother a clue about how he could continue to practise doing homework on his own.

★ ★ ★

Demonstrating skills is not only useful because it helps children develop a clear picture of what it means to have a skill. It also helps them pick up ideas about how they might practise it.

We will soon go on to talk about how the child can actually practise the skill, but before that, let's have a word about why it is so important for the child to go public and to let people know about the skill she is learning.

Step 10

Going public

Inform people what skill the child is learning

People can encourage the child only if they know what it is that he is learning

The expression 'going public' means here that we let people know about the skill the child is learning. The benefit of this is that when people know the child is learning a new skill, they can encourage her and help her to learn it.

Andy was a bright six-year-old boy who had no friends, always played alone and avoided contact with other children. At the school he attended, all the children were learning personal skills. Not surprisingly, Andy's skill was to learn to play with other children. Every child had a poster on the classroom wall showing what skills they were learning. After having seen Andy's poster, a mother of one of Andy's classmates approached Andy's mother and suggested that Andy come to play with her son who was often lonely and needed someone to play with. Without 'going public', this opportunity would perhaps never have been presented.

It is far easier to talk about skills to be learned than about problems to be removed

Children usually dislike their issues being talked about publicly. For them, having problems means there is something wrong with them, and that in turn tends to provoke feelings of shame. However, the same is not true when we talk with children about skills they need to learn. There is no stigma attached to learning skills. Children know that everyone needs to do so. Indeed, learning skills is something children tend to be proud of.

What is true of children is true of their parents too. Parents prefer to talk about skills their children need to learn rather than about problems with their children. This is no surprise, taking into account the fact that we live in a culture which tends to blame parents for all their children's difficulties.

Many years ago I worked as a general practitioner in a rural health care centre when a mother came to see me with her six-year-old daughter. While the mother was trying to explain to me what the issue was – the girl soiled her underwear – the girl was so ashamed that she tried to prevent her mother from speaking by covering the mother's mouth with her hand. The situation might have been much easier for the child had I known how to shift from talking about 'the problem' to talking about the skill the girl needed to learn.

Several years later, at a training seminar, I met a girl of the same age with the same trouble:

Natalie had the habit of soiling her underwear. She stared at the floor as her mother explained things to me. As soon as I had an idea of the issue, I shifted the conversation from the problem to the skill that Natalie needed to learn.

'Have there been times when Natalie has been able to hold on until she could get to the toilet?' I asked.

'Oh, yes,' said the mother. 'In fact only a while ago there was a period of two weeks when she used the toilet every day and did not soil her underwear even once. But now the problem is back and she is soiling again.'

I turned to Natalie: 'Wow! Is that true? Were you really able to do it in the toilet every day for two weeks in a row? That's quite an accomplishment, I must say. How on earth did you do it? How were you able to make it happen?'

Natalie looked up from the floor and then whispered something in her mother's ear.

'May I know what she told you?' I asked the mother.

'Natalie says that she doesn't know how she did it,' the mother said.

I looked at Natalie and said, 'Guess what? I think I know. I know why you were able to do it in the toilet for so long. Do you want to know, too?'

Natalie became curious. As she had nodded her affirmation, I began to tell her about a special fairy that helps children learn to go to the toilet. I explained to her that I believed the 'toilet fairy' must have been helping her during those two successful weeks. I noticed that Natalie was amused by the idea of the toilet fairy helping her go to the toilet and soon we were both sitting on the floor, together drawing a picture of the toilet fairy on a large sheet of paper.

Once we had completed the drawing, the discussion shifted naturally towards talk about how Natalie could learn to go to the toilet every day again. Natalie was allowed to feel proud of having been able to go to the toilet for two weeks in a row, and happy for having the toilet fairy as her supporter.

Going public reduces prejudice

When we talk about skills to be learned rather than problems to be overcome, greater openness becomes possible. Openness in turn makes it possible for the child to have many supporters. In addition, focusing on skills also has a favourable effect on the way in which the adults involved treat the child.

There is a famous experiment, done years ago, which examined the effect of teachers' presuppositions on children's academic achievement. In the school where the experiment was carried out, all the children starting school were given an aptitude test. The researchers did not look at the results but divided the children arbitrarily into different groups. Then they went to the teachers and told them (incorrectly) which of the children were particularly talented and which of them were untalented.

The researchers then left the school and returned some time later to test the children again. They found that the children they had arbitrarily labelled talented ('you can expect much from this child') had done a lot better than the children they had labelled untalented ('don't expect too much from this child'). This experiment opened our eyes to see that our expectations influence not only the way we treat children but also the way they behave.

This same phenomenon – 'the expectation effect', if you will – is also at play when children experience problems. If a child has a difficulty and everyone seems to think there is little that can be done about it, a pessimistic view of the possibilities for overcoming the difficulty infects the child. She begins to think, 'I am like this and there's little I can do about it.' On the other hand, if people around the child think in terms of her needing to learn a skill, and they show they have confidence, the child will be affected by this attitude. She will think, 'I have a skill to learn, and even if it takes me a while, in the end I will learn it.'

How widely to go public?

In saying all this, I am not arguing that whenever a child is learning a skill the whole world should know about it. There are many situations in which it is quite enough that the project of learning a skill is made public only within the family. I talked earlier about Noah, the fourteen-year-old boy who stole money from his family. The skill he needed to learn was to become honest and trustworthy again. As he had never stolen money from anybody outside the family, it was easy to make the decision that his learning of the skill would not be publicised outside the family.

When we think about how widely to inform people about a skill, we may want to take into consideration how public the issue is. The ground rule is that if the issue is public and everybody knows about it anyway, we should consider making the learning of the skill public as well. In other words, if people are already talking about the child, it is better that they talk about what skill he is learning than about what problems he has.

As an example, let's imagine a child we will call Sandy. She is eight years old and so extremely shy that she refuses to talk with anyone except members of her immediate family. She doesn't even speak with her teacher at school. This behaviour is called 'selective mutism' in child psychiatry. At school everyone knows about the issue. Nobody talks about it openly but it is discussed in the hallways and behind the scenes. The children find Sandy's muteness strange and the teachers are worried about her. They know she goes to some sort of therapy but they don't know anything about what happens there. All in all, it would be fair to say that a curtain of mystery and secretiveness is hanging over Sandy's muteness. And that makes things even more difficult for her.

Now let's suppose we want to use Kids' Skills to help Sandy. First of all we wouldn't concentrate on her being mute, but on identifying the skill she needs to develop. Sandy would probably agree with us that for her to overcome her shyness or muteness she would need to develop the skill – or courage, in this case – to talk with people outside her immediate family. Sandy would be asked to give a name to this courage. She might, for example, decide to call it 'the chatting courage'. She would then choose a power creature, examine the benefits of developing that courage, ask a number of people, including some friends, to be her supporters, and so on. When it is time for Sandy to demonstrate how she behaves once she has developed her 'chatting courage', she could do with the help of a hand puppet. The puppet could be of her teacher, a friend of hers, or anyone else she wishes to learn to talk with. Finally plans would be made with Sandy about how she would practise this courage.

She would probably want to practise in a way that allows her to proceed in small steps. Perhaps she would like to start by having conversations with imaginary people, or role-play with hand puppets. Then she could try chatting with a particular person over the Internet, or on the phone, and then later she could try to talk to someone face-to-face. Little by little she would extend the circle of adults and friends she talks with until the issue is resolved.

An important part of this approach is that the project would be made known to the school. Sandy's teachers, as well as her classmates, would know about the 'chatting courage thing', and about the way in which Sandy was trying to develop that courage. Instead of the mysterious and secretive 'problem', there would be a girl learning a skill that everyone can talk about openly, and in a positive spirit. An atmosphere would be created that makes it possible for everyone – teachers as well as classmates – to help and encourage Sandy as she learns to talk with everyone.

How to go public?

Going public can be done in a number of ways. If you are a teacher and you want to use Kids' Skills with your pupils, you may want to consider hanging a skills chart on the wall of the classroom. Our 'Skills Chart' is a simple table: in the first column, the names of all the pupils in the class are listed; in the second column, the skills the pupils are learning; in the third column, the names the children have given to their skills; in the fourth column, brief descriptions of how the child wants to be reminded (if she forgets her skill); and in the last column, the names of supporters. Such a table allows everyone, at a glance, to get a good idea of the skills the children are learning.

A practical way to go public is to use a Kids' Skills workbook with pages for each step of the Kids' Skills process and also some room for supporters to write their words of encouragement. A convenient alternative to the workbook is a poster that has most of the main steps of Kids' Skills on it. On the following page you can see a commercially available example of this poster*.

* Selected Kids' Skills products are available from www.stlukes.org.au/resources

Kids' Skills

1. Convert problems into skills the child can learn.

2. Talk with the child about what skill you want him to learn.

3. Help the child see the benefits of the skill, for others as well as for himself.

4. Let the child give a name to the skill.

5. Ask the child to choose a power animal that helps him learn the skill.

6. Help the child find supporters.

7. Ask the child's supporters to tell him why they are confident he will learn the skill.

8. Make a plan with the child about how to celebrate when he has learned the skill.

9. Ask the child to demonstrate to you how he will behave when he has learned the skill.

10. Help the child tell people what skill he is going to learn.

11. Let the child practice the skill by giving him opportunities to show how skilful he already is.

12. Let the child tell you how he wants to be reminded if he forgets the skill.

13. When it is time to celebrate, ask the child to thank all the supporters for their help.

14. Give the child an opportunity to teach the skill to other children.

15. Discuss with the child the next skill he will learn.

Information: www.kidsskills.org   Illustrations: Kai Kujasalo   © Helsinki Brief Therapy Institute

Available from www.kidsskills.org

We have now come a long way in familiarising ourselves with the steps of Kids' Skills. We have learned how to convert problems into skills, and how to reach agreement with the child about the right skill to learn. We know how to help children see what having the skill will do, both for them and other people, and we can inspire children to find personal names for their skills. We understand how power creatures can help children as they are struggling to learn their skills, and we can appreciate the importance of having supporters who are willing to encourage children while they are practising. We know how to boost children's confidence, and how to give them an extra surge of motivation by making plans with them about how acquiring the skill is to be celebrated. We have learned how to make sure children understand what having the skill means in actual practice, and in this chapter we have found out about the benefits of making Kids' Skills projects public.

But there is a critical part of Kids' Skills that we haven't talked about yet. It is said that 'well planned is half done', but no one learns skills by planning alone. For children to learn skills they need to practise them. That will be the topic of the next section.

Practising the skill

Agree with the child about how she will practise the skill

Practice makes perfect

For children to learn their skills they need to practise. Therefore we adults need to find ways in which they can exercise their skills. And for their practice to yield results, it needs to happen frequently and for a long enough period.

In most cases finding a way for the child to practise his skill is easy but in some cases it requires further thought. Let's say the child's difficulty is that he doesn't know how to tie his shoelaces. Obviously then, tying his shoelaces is the skill he needs to learn. It is also easy to come up with ideas about how he could practise that skill. For example, he might start by tying simple knots with a rope and after learning that he might go on to tying similar knots on a thinner rope and so on, until he is ready to practise tying his shoelaces.

The best way to practise
a skill is to perform it

When children learn skills spontaneously they often use a learning method that could be called 'showing', 'demonstrating' or 'performing'. We all know how they do it. A child asks her parents, or other adults, to watch her repeatedly while she does something which is difficult and which she is proud of. For example, when children learn to do somersaults or to ride a bike, they often ask their parents to watch them. 'Watch me', 'Look here', 'You're not watching', 'You promised to watch', 'Just once more, please look!' they cry out, requesting adults to admire how skilful they are. Performing skills and receiving admiration from adults are essential ingredients in helping children learn. In fact, from the child's point of view, learning skills means that you do something difficult while adults show their admiration by exclamations such as 'Wow', 'Excellent!' or 'Look how good you are!'

Gary was five years old and the skill he was learning at preschool was to put his winter clothes on quickly when going out after lunch. He himself had named his skill 'the speed of light' and he practised the skill by performing it every Friday morning. His performance consisted of standing beside a pile of clothes and then, at the count of 'ready steady go', he would quickly put on his winter clothes while the group encouraged him as if he were engaged in a sports activity. In addition to performing his skill in this ritualised manner, he also had the opportunity to show his skill every day when the children were going out after lunch. For Gary the practice was a fun game but it helped him learn to put his clothes on quickly.

Let the child come up with
ideas for how to practise the skill

When we find it difficult to come up with a way in which the child can practise a skill we may need to be inventive. Fortunately, children are particularly creative when it comes to thinking about how to practise skills. In fact, children are born with the talent for inventing games to practise things they observe adults or older children doing. With that talent, children usually have no trouble inventing a role-play, performance or game that allows them to practise their specific skills.

Ten-year-old Arthur was troubled by anxiety: he never wanted to leave his mother for fear that something awful would happen to her while she was gone. Arthur himself was also keen on overcoming his fear, so it was easy to agree with him that the skill he needed to learn was the ability to calmly allow his mother to go out. When I asked Arthur how he could practise his skill, he spontaneously came up with the intelligent idea that his mother would go out with the dog while he was watching her through the window.

'What a wonderful idea,' I said to Arthur. 'I'm sure it would work. I suspect that once you've done that a couple of times with your mum, you'll have no trouble at all letting your mum go out with the dog while you watch her through the window. And then you'll need to make the exercise more difficult. How would you do that? What would be the next step in your training program?'

'The next' step will be that Mum goes around the corner and disappears for a while from my sight,' Arthur explained. As we continued our conversation, Arthur drew up an excellent step-by-step plan for practising the art of being separated from his mother without panicking.

I might have been able to design a similar step-by-step training program for Arthur myself, but I doubt that it would have worked as well as the plan he came up with. I am convinced that allowing children to participate actively in the making of their own training programs yields far better results than any programs we parents or professionals create for them.

How often should the child practise the skill?

The child should perform his skill often enough and for as long as necessary for the skill to become ingrained – to become a habit, a part of his personality, so to speak. How frequently should we ask children to practise their skills? That depends. A useful rule of thumb is that children should practise their skills at least once a day but the truth is that some skills require much more practice than others.

Felix was wetting his bed. The skill he was going to learn was being able to keep dry though the night. To learn this skill he practised the art of becoming better at controlling his bladder muscle. Felix practised his skill every time he went to the toilet, using the so-called stop-and-start exercise, which required him to start then stop urinating three times during each visit to the toilet. Felix became a master of stop-and-start urinating within a week, after which he was ready to take the next step, which in this case was being able to perform the same skill while lying down. For this purpose the family borrowed a bedpan from a local hospital. It didn't take many rehearsals before Felix was so proficient that he was able to do it with his eyes closed – even in his sleep.

Small steps

As you would have noticed from reading the examples in this book, when children learn skills with the help of Kids' Skills they do it progressively, starting with easy exercises and then making the exercises gradually more difficult. For example, if the child is to acquire the skill of playing by herself for a period of time, she would start by practising playing on her own for just a few minutes, and after having succeeded with that she would move on to learning to play on her own for slightly longer, and so on. Likewise, if a child who is very picky about food is learning to expand her choices by tasting other kinds of food, she might start by tasting various kinds of exotic fruits or different flavoured yoghurts. Having succeeded with that, she might move on to tasting different vegetables, and when she begins to feel more comfortable with trying new foods, she might move on to tasting food that had previously been particularly difficult for her to eat.

Jenny was six years old, and she became unhappy whenever her mother was to leave her at the preschool. Jenny demanded her mother walk her up the stairs to the second floor of the preschool and when her mother was about to leave Jenny would demand that she stay by crying desperately and begging. The issue was serious, as the mother's boss had already reprimanded her for being late for work so often.

The skill that Jenny was learning was to depart from her mother calmly. What it meant in practice was that Jenny would be able to let her mother leave for work with the words 'Bye for now, Mum' or 'See you later'. Jenny practised this skill of hers with the help of the following role-play.

In this game two of Jenny's friends – her peer supporters – played the role of adults. One of the friends stood at the bottom of the stairs playing the role of her mother, the other stood at the top of the stairs playing the role of the teacher. Jenny played herself. The game started with Jenny standing with her make-believe mother at the bottom of the stairs. She then said 'Bye now, Mum' to her make-believe mother, climbed the stairs, and gave a hug to the make-believe teacher standing at the top of the stairs. Jenny liked the exercise very much and was ready to try to do the same with her real mother the next day.

The following morning her mother called the preschool and informed the staff that she would bring Jenny an hour later than usual. When they arrived, Jenny's peer supporters were eagerly waiting for them, ready to try the 'Bye now, Mum' game with Jenny's real mother. After two rounds of the game, with Jenny's real mother at the bottom of the stairs and both of her peer supporters playing the role of the teacher at the top of the stairs, Jenny let her mother go to work without any protest at all. She had learned the skill of separating from her mother calmly.

Success diary

Small children like to make up role-plays to practise skills, but the same is not always true for bigger children, to whom the idea of a role-play may seem too childish.

In such cases we would consider replacing role-play with what could be called a 'success log' or 'success diary'. This means that we do not create any artificial situations for the child to demonstrate or perform his skill, but we simply keep a record of all those real-life situations in which the child behaves in accordance with it. Say a twelve-year-old boy is learning to ask for permission to talk in class by raising his hand, rather than shouting out. The boy might not fancy the idea of role-playing the skill. Instead, he might like the idea that his teacher and his supporters would take on the task of keeping a record of all those instances where he raises his hand when he wants to say something in class. The important thing here is to create a context in which the child has experiences of success and receives positive feedback for those successes.

Eleven-year-old Ariel was learning to take care of packing his school bag in the evening so as to have the right books for school the next day. He exercised his skill by trying to pack the right books into his school bag every evening. The teacher had divided the pupils of the class into supporter groups consisting of four children whose task was to support and encourage each other in learning their skills. The other members of Ariel's supporter group checked his bag every morning to see if he had succeeded in performing his skill. If all the right books were found, his supporters wrote a comment about it in his log, which was a sheet of paper on the classroom wall with one column for the date and another one for statements such as 'All the right books in the bag'. Even if just a single item was missing from his bag, nothing was to be written on his log sheet. At the end of every week the teacher examined Ariel's log sheet, publicly admired his progress and acknowledged the members of his supporter group for having helped Ariel succeed in learning his skill.

Making sure the child has energy to keep on practising

For children to have the motivation to practise their skills, they should be practising in a way that is fun and rewarding. We can ensure that the practice is rewarding by arranging for the children to get plenty of attention and admiration every time they perform their skills or exhibit other signs of progress.

If children are practising their skills at day care, at school or any other place caring for children, it is important to see to it that not only adults but also the other children in the group take part in showing admiration for the child's progress. At Keula day care centre, when all the children perform their skills on Friday mornings the teachers as well as all the other children in the group show their appreciation by cheering and applauding the performing child.

Triple praise

When the child's supporters see her acting out her skill they can give her compliments, such as 'You learn quickly', 'See how good you are', 'There you go' or 'I'm proud of you!' There are myriad ways of showing appreciation to a child who is performing her skill. We compliment children for performing their skills to give them an opportunity to feel proud of their progress. It is the feeling of pride that feeds children's motivation to go on practising until the day they master their skills well enough to warrant a celebration.

Triple praise is a fine way of supporting children when they perform their skills. It consists of the following three parts:

1. **Exclamation of wonder**
   Show admiration with words, facial expressions and gestures and say to the child something like: 'Wow!', 'Great!', 'Excellent!', 'Unbelievable!', 'Extraordinary!', 'I can't believe it!' or 'Well done again!'

2. **Declaration of difficulty**
   Let the child know you understand that the thing the child has done is not easy. Say, for example: 'That's not easy at all', 'That must be difficult', 'I don't think I could do that', 'Some people think that's easy but I know it isn't' or 'How did you learn to do that so quickly?'

3. **Request for explanation**
   Finally, with genuine curiosity in your voice, ask the child to explain how he did it. You may say, for example: 'How on earth did you do that?' or 'Now you have to explain to me how you do that.'

Try the 'triple praise' with children in various situations and you'll see with your own eyes how effective it is for giving children the feeling of pride and mastery.

Praising through the grapevine

Another highly effective way of praising the child is what could be called 'praising through the grapevine'. Here we don't praise children face-to-face but to a third person while they overhear us. Children (and, of course, adults too) are delighted to hear that people are saying good things about them to each other.

Not long ago I was talking with my father on the mobile phone in the car. I have a hands-free system installed, which means that everyone sitting in the car can hear the voice of the person speaking at the other end of the line. My father began to praise my daughter, unaware that she was sitting next to me hearing every word he said. I could see, out of the corner of my eye, a big smile appearing on my daughter's face. When I finally got the chance, I told my father that she was sitting next to me and that she could hear what he was saying. 'Is that so?' my father said with his humorous tone of voice. 'In that case, tell her that I take it back, that none of what I said is true.' My daughter got the message and burst out laughing with me.

Children as well as adults seem to be more receptive to positive feedback when it is passed on to them in an indirect way – that is, when it reaches their ears through a third person or messenger. We all like to hear a person telling us positive things about ourselves, but don't we like it even more when a person is telling us that *someone else* has said something positive about us? This is why we should take every opportunity to express praise for our children to other people while our children can hear us, and to relate to them anything positive that we have heard other people say about them.

- Mother to father while the child hears: 'Mike has been behaving so well today. You should be proud of him.'

- Father to mother while the child can hear: 'I have good news. Do you want to hear what the teacher told me about Mandy today?'

- Teacher to a child: 'Sarah [another teacher at the same school] told me this morning that you were able to listen to the story she told from the beginning to the end without interrupting her even once. That's quite an achievement for you. How did you do that?'

- Mother to grandmother while the child is eavesdropping from the back seat of the car: 'When I went to pick Sam up from school today, the teacher said so many good things about him that I didn't know what to say. Among other things she said that…'

Praising is a team sport

Showing admiration for the child works best when all those who are close to the child join forces and do it together. This is, however, easier said than done, particularly in cases when children perform their skills in one environment, say at school, but they do not yet perform the same skill in another environment, say at home.

Willie used to swear a lot. Persuaded that swearing was something he had to get rid of, he agreed to learn to talk inoffensively. He made rapid progress, in fact within a week or so he was already talking quite courteously at school, without any swearwords or unkind remarks. When Willie's mother came to pick him up, one of the teachers went over to tell her the good news. 'You'll love to hear this,' the teacher said. 'He's been speaking like an angel all week. No bad words, no nasty expressions. He's been a true gentleman. Isn't it great?'

The teacher expected Willie's mother to be delighted about her son's progress, but what happened was to the contrary. She seemed quite disappointed. She looked Willie in the eye and said, with irritation in her voice: 'I don't get it. You behave like a gentleman here at school but at home you talk to me like you hate me, or something. Why can't you talk in a nice way at home as well? You seem to be able to do it here, so what's the problem? I really don't get it!'

A moment before, Willie had been proud of his achievement, but his mother's words blew away his pride. He didn't say a word. He just walked away to join his friends who were playing ball. That evening, he didn't even try to talk politely to his mother.

One can easily sympathise with Willie's mother. What she said was understandable, but not very helpful. After all, hearing that your 'difficult' child behaves well while he is being taken care of by someone else is good news and bad news at the same time. The good news is that your child *can* behave well. The bad news is that this can be taken to mean that the problem is not with your child, but with you. Therefore all those who care for children need to be mindful of how to pass on good news, or news about progress, to others caring for the same children. We need to be aware of the fact that even if the child is making progress while he is with us, he may still be displaying the problematic behaviour in another environment. This situation needs to be dealt with in a sensitive manner if we want to avoid sending out the message that the problem must be 'someone's fault'.

Willie's teacher took the incident up with the mother the next day. 'I think I can understand how you must feel,' she began. 'I mean, it may not feel all that good to learn that Willie is talking politely here at school while he is still being rude to you at home. However, when we report his progress here at school, we need you to compliment him, because we think that's the best way of helping him to expand his learning and to start to talk politely to you at home as well. Would you feel OK about saying something like "Well done" or "Mum is proud of you" next time one of us tells you about his progress? That would probably be the best way to get him to learn to behave at home too.'

Willie's mother understood the idea and promised to try. The next day when she came to pick him up, the teacher approached her and said, 'Willie hasn't been using any foul language today. He's been a gentleman.' His mother was just about to start scolding him for not behaving at home when she remembered. She turned to Willie and said, 'I'm so happy to hear that. I'm so proud of you!'

You could see from Willie's face that he was delighted with his mother's words. That same evening, his mother said that Willie had at least tried to speak more respectfully to her.

Children acquire new skills quickly, but learning new behaviours happens rarely without any incident. As the saying goes, two steps forward are followed by one step back. How do we deal with situations in which children experience setbacks, or they forget all about the skills they are learning and temporarily slip back to their old behaviour? This dilemma will be the topic of our next section.

Creating reminders

Let the child tell you how he wants others to react if he forgets his skill

It's better to see a slip as skills being temporarily forgotten, rather than problems returning

Seven-year-old Neil, who had a mild intellectual disability, had difficulty in sitting up straight. Whether he was sitting at the dining table or at his desk, it didn't take long for him to start sliding down in his chair until he was practically lying on the table. Due to his bad posture he was often unable to complete tasks given to him by the teacher, and at lunch he ate so untidily that he not only messed up the table but also his clothes. Neil's personal assistant at school spoke to him about this.

'Neil, I'd like you to tell me how you want me to point out when you forget to sit up straight, and you begin to slide down on the table again. What do you want me to tell you when that happens?'

'You can call me "Donald",' said Neil.

'All right, let's try it then,' said the assistant. 'Go ahead and start slumping on the table and I'll call you "Donald" so we can see how it works for you.'

The magic word 'Donald' had been invented by Neil himself and worked well, so his personal assistant used it whenever there was a need to remind him to sit up straight.

Dealing with frustration and disappointment

When children are learning abilities with the help of Kid' Skills, sooner or later the day will arrive when the child forgets the skill she is trying to acquire and slips back to the very behaviour she is learning to overcome. Such a slip is worth our attention as it plays a pivotal role in the learning process. At best, slipping gives an extra boost to the child's will to learn her skill, while at worst it demoralises the child to the point that she gives up trying.

We all know how children react when they become demoralised, when they lose their confidence and faith in themselves. This is when we hear them saying things like:

- 'I told you I'll never learn!'

- 'This is a waste of time. It won't work anyway!'

- 'I'm no good. I can't do it!'

Forgetting the skill poses a threat of demoralisation not only for the child, but also for the adults caring for the child. When adults become demoralised they may express their disappointment by saying things like:

- 'Oh Johnny, not you again.'

- 'Didn't we just agree that you would...?'

- 'There you go again! You're not even trying.'

- Or even, 'Nothing works with you, not even Kids' Skills!'

The feelings of disappointment and demoralisation experienced by adults, even when not verbally expressed, have a tendency to be passed on to children, adding to their discouragement.

How to remind the child

In Kids' Skills slipping is viewed as an expected part of a normal learning curve. Keeping this in mind will not only help us avoid feelings of discouragement when the child experiences setbacks, but will also prepare us in advance for such situations. Bring up the subject of slipping with the child and make an agreement with him about how to deal with such a situation. Let the child be responsible for telling us how he wants other people to respond to situations in which he slips, or temporarily loses his skill.

- 'If you sometimes forget to use your skill, would you like me to tell you something or would you prefer me to show you a sign of some sort instead?'

- 'What do you want your parents to tell you if you happen to forget your skill?'

- 'How do you want your classmates to remind you if they notice that you have forgotten your skill and are about to slip back to the old behaviour?'

When the child has decided how she wants other people to remind her if she forgets her skill, we can test her suggestion to see how it works. For example, if the child wants us to remind her of her skill by saying the name of her power creature, we can role-play a situation in which she forgets her skill and starts to display the behaviour she is learning to overcome. We then remind her by saying the name of her power creature, while she shows us how she gets back on track by performing her skill.

Having children tell us how they want other people to remind them of their skills at times of slipping helps children perceive their supporters' reactions as gestures of help rather than scolding. When children request us to remind them in a particular way, they are actively cooperating with us in finding a solution to the challenge of slipping. After all, a requested reminder is not criticism – it is an act of helpfulness.

Children can take care of reminding each other

If you are a teacher and you use Kids' Skills with your class, you will probably not have enough time to remind all the children about their skills every time they slip and forget them. Instead of even trying to take responsibility for reminding the children, you might want to consider sharing the task with the pupils, by asking them to take care of reminding each other when they slip. Here again, it is useful to divide the pupils into peer support groups and to have the peer supporters take responsibility for reminding each other.

With this arrangement you would not remind children of their skills when you notice that they slip. Instead you would turn to the child's peer supporters and ask them to do it for you. This arrangement works because you don't ask the children to criticise each other for forgetting their skills; you ask them to kindly remind each other in the exact way they themselves asked to be reminded in those situations.

When children practise their skills for a period of time and they overcome their slips with dignity, they sooner or later learn their skills. Then it will be time to arrange for the celebration. How this celebration should be arranged and what should happen at the celebration is the topic of our next section.

Step 13

Celebrating success

When the child has acquired the skill, it is time to celebrate and to give her an opportunity to acknowledge all those who helped her learn it

Acknowledging others for their help is like sharing pieces of a magic cake – the more you share, the bigger and the more beautiful the cake becomes

When children have practised for a time and they have repeatedly shown that they have mastered their skills – not only in a role-play but also in real-life situations – and that they are, if requested, able to teach their skills to other people, it is time to arrange for the celebration.

Usually it is easy to say when children have acquired their skills. Say a child is learning to tie his shoelaces, to use the toilet, to ride a bike without the training wheels, or to be friendly with his peers, it is easy to judge whether the skill has been acquired or not. Also, children are usually quite capable of telling us whether they have already mastered a skill or still need some training.

However, sometimes there is a need to have a discussion about whether a child already possesses a skill or not. For example, if Jason has been learning the skill of playing cooperatively with other children, it may not be all that simple to determine when the time is ripe for him to have his celebration.

When judging whether Jason has already acquired the skill of playing cooperatively with other children, we might want to start with Jason and ask him what he thinks. In addition, we would probably want to talk to some people who see him interacting with other children on a daily basis to find out what they think. A teacher who uses Kids' Skills put it succinctly: 'A child has learned his skill when he himself, and other people as well, agree that he has learned it.'

What if children do not learn their skills?

Children usually learn their skills within a couple of weeks, or a few months at the most. If not, we try to find out why this is the case. One possible reason is that the skill the child is learning is too big or too complex for her. In that case we consider revising the skill and splitting it into smaller components, then finding agreement with the child that she concentrate on learning one of the components rather than the whole skill. You will find more information about splitting complex skills into smaller parts in the first step of Kids' Skills (see page 16).

Another possible explanation for why children sometimes have trouble learning their skills is that they haven't fully understood what benefits having that skill will bring for them, or anybody else. In this case we go back and re-examine the benefits of having those skills.

A third possibility is that children haven't had enough chance to practise their skills. In the ninth step of Kids' Skills we talked about the importance of making sure the child has ample opportunities to perform his skill, and it was pointed out that practising the skill should be something the child experiences as fun and rewarding.

One more possible explanation for children not learning their skills within a reasonable time frame is that all the adults caring for them are not cooperating in helping them to learn – that is, not all the key adults are participating in supporting and encouraging the children in their attempts to acquire their skills.

The following example, told by the British school nurse Anne Turner, is a fine illustration of the importance of all key adults pulling in the same direction:

I have used Kids' Skills with many children and usually the child's behaviour changes very quickly to what his or her parents and teachers want. The method, being very simple, does indeed seem to be a very effective process.

But not all children doing it are quick to get the hang of it. For example, it took Bob quite some time to crack his particular skill of learning not to 'touch' other children. The school continued to be very concerned about his behaviour in relation to other children, and although some improvements did occur, it did get back to the point of the headmaster having to consider the possibility of permanent exclusion, and in fact Bob did get excluded from the school whilst doing Kids' Skills.

At this stage Bob was spending most of his time in the head teacher's office doing his schoolwork. I contacted Andrew Duggan [a Kids' Skills therapist], not knowing quite what was supposed to happen now. A meeting was arranged with the school, with Andrew explaining that Bob needed to be in an environment where he had the opportunity to 'show' his skill. At this point the headmistress had a number of parents coming to see her about Bob's behaviour and the effects it was having on their children, but she still had enough faith to return Bob to the class setting. We also arranged a meeting with the parents again as they had not written any comments in Bob's Kids' Skills workbook.

At the meeting with Bob's dad, we agreed that he would take time in the evening to look at the book with his son. This would not always be easy as he also had a younger son who was a handful, and his wife worked long hours. The Health Visitor – who had agreed to be present at this meeting – and myself would visit the dad to give him some support.

This provided a turning point and with the dad's support now included in the package, a difference in behaviour was increasingly noticed and we had a celebration, which Bob thoroughly enjoyed.

It is now over a year since Bob started on his first Kids' Skills project. On his third skill, the ability to listen, with Mum and Dad on board from the outset, Bob's improvement in this area was quick and noticeable.

Other changes for Bob are that before starting Kids' Skills, Bob could not play in his own street for fear of being bullied, and now he has friends he can play with in his street. Could this be attributed to Kids' Skills? Who can tell? Personally, I feel that Kids' Skills has made an impact not only on his behaviour in class, but also in the playground, and therefore it would be logical that it would also affect his behaviour with other children out of school.

The meaning of the celebration

Before long the child learns her skill and the time has come to arrange for the celebration, as planned in the ninth step. The celebration works as a carrot for the child, but it is much more than that.

In addition to being a reward for children to anticipate, the celebration is also a kind of press conference or public briefing, a social event to inform people that children have acquired the skills they have been learning. It is a kind of ritual that has positive effects on the children as well as on their social environment. It is a turning point for children, a moment in time when they transform from apprentice to master. After this event people in the surrounding environment can expect that the child is able to perform the skill not only in a role-play but in actual situations as well. That does not, however, mean that children are never supposed to slip again. There's certainly room for some slipping and sliding even after the celebration.

When I was a teenager I learned judo. I remember the time when I took the test for the first grade, the yellow belt. It meant that I was to perform my newly acquired skills of falling and throwing others correctly in front of a jury. I passed the exam and got my first belt. It didn't mean that I would never again do those things in the wrong way but that I had progressed to a level that allowed me to go on and start learning new techniques.

Acknowledging others

That children acknowledge their supporters for having helped them learn their skills is an essential ingredient of celebrating success in Kids' Skills. This means that we talk with children to help them become aware of how various people helped, encouraged and supported them along the way. As children become aware of how others have helped them, they can begin to feel grateful, which in turn makes it possible for them to express their gratitude in one way or another.

The following is an example of a conversation with a schoolchild whose teacher is helping him to become aware of how his supporters contributed to his success:

Liam has learned to behave well in class. The teacher says, 'You have learned to behave well and everyone admires you for your progress. You've done a great job. Who were the ones who helped you along the way?'

'Nick and Oi,' Liam says.

'How did Nick and Oi help you?'

'They reminded me whenever I forgot my skill and they also kept a record for me of the times when I was able to behave well.'

'Wow, that must have been useful for you,' says the teacher, and she suggests that he shake hands with Nick and Oi to thank them for their help. Liam does it with pleasure. The teacher goes on: 'Anybody else you could mention? Has anybody else supported you in some way? Your parents, for example?'

'Mum did,' says Liam.

'In what way?'

Liam thinks for a moment and then says, 'She explained to me why it's so important to learn to behave well at school.'

'That's great,' said the teacher. 'What you are saying is that your mum helped you to see why the struggle was worthwhile. Let's write that down in your workbook. I'm sure your mum will be delighted to read it and to learn that you, too, think that her efforts have helped you. Anybody else? Was there someone else who gave you a hand or supported you in some way? How about me? Was there anything I did that was helpful to you?'

'Of course,' said Liam, surprised by his teacher's direct question, but he went on to explain how the teacher too had helped him learn his skill.

The positive effects of thanking others

Acknowledging others is not simply a formality but one of the most important steps of Kids' Skills. It is a step that gives the child an opportunity to experience gratitude. At the same time it delights all those who have contributed to supporting the child by giving them a feeling that they have done something worthwhile, something that has been of use to the child.

The feeling of gratitude, and particularly the act of expressing it, is one of the most important social skills. To succeed in life, we all need other people's help and support. The ability to feel and express gratitude increases our likelihood of getting help and support from other people in the future, which in turn increases our chances of succeeding in whatever it is we are doing in our lives.

The act of a child acknowledging or thanking her supporters for their contribution affects people positively. For supporters it feels good to be acknowledged by a child for their contributions. It is a well-deserved reward that makes them feel their efforts have been worthwhile and increases their willingness to continue to support the child. If we want our children to become aware of how other people help them in life and to learn to acknowledge those contributions, we have to train them to do just that, so that it becomes something that comes naturally to them.

All of us who work with children need to hear, once in a while, that our work brings results, spreads joy, and helps develop competence in children. After all, is there anything more rewarding than having a child come to you and sincerely thank you for having contributed to his learning a skill that you both know is useful and important for his life?

It might seem that the process of learning a new skill ends when the children have acquired their skills, celebrated their success and acknowledged their supporters. But this is not the case in Kids' Skills. The circle is completed only after children have taken two more steps: the step of teaching their skill to someone else, and the step of moving on to the next skill.

Step 14

Passing the skill on to others

Encourage the child to teach the new skill to another child

The best way to learn something is to teach it to someone else

Several years ago I was at an international psychotherapy congress in the United States. One of the presenters of the congress, Dr Terry Tofoya, a North American psychologist and healer, told a Native American Indian teaching story that made a strong impression on me. The story was about an unhappy girl named Ayayesh, who was looked down upon by everyone because she didn't do anything useful for anybody in the village.

The unhappy Ayayesh left the village and went to the wilderness. There she met various animals, each of which taught her some skill she could use to do something useful in her village. For example, when Ayayesh met the snake, the snake taught her how to weave the zigzag pattern on its back, and when Ayayesh came upon the owl, it taught her how to weave another pattern with the eyes of the owl.

When Ayayesh returned to her village after her long journey in the wilderness, she surprised the villagers by weaving the most beautiful patterns ever seen there.

At this point Dr Tofoya stopped drumming and asked all of us in the audience if we thought the story had come to an end. He then answered his own question by saying: 'Usually people brought up in Western civilisation feel that the story ends when Ayayesh returns to her village after having learned to weave beautiful patterns, but according to our tradition, the tradition of the Native Americans, the story does not end quite yet.' Having said that, Dr Tofoya began pounding on his drum again and told the end of the story. In this ending Ayayesh was asked to teach her newly learned skills to the other villagers to make the new knowledge available to everyone in the village.

In the tradition of Native American Indians, as well as many other traditional cultures on our planet, learning is seen as a circle that starts with ignorance, continues with learning, and ends only when the person has disseminated the learning to the tribe. To know something, it is not enough just to know it. You also have to be able to teach it to others.

The teacher learns too

Passing skills on to others serves the community, but it also serves the person who teaches his skill to others. It is well known that one of the most efficient ways to learn a thing is to teach it to someone else. Therefore in Kids' Skills we try to arrange for children to have opportunities to pass their skills on to other children. Doing that helps children reinforce their skills, thus diminishing the risk of slipping.

Karen had learned to calm down for the obligatory afternoon nap and she had moved on to learning her next skill. When the children went for their afternoon nap and the teacher was reading a fairytale to them, Dan, who was a year younger than Karen, started to create havoc and was trying to drag some of the other children along too. Karen looked at the nurse and said, 'Do you remember, I was just like that before?' She then turned to the boy who was creating havoc and said, 'Look here, all you need to do is lie down like this, see, put your hands by your side and look at the ceiling, and relax. It's easy. You can do it.' The boy looked at Karen with amazement and did exactly as she had told him.

Acknowledging others improves reputation and increases appreciation

An interesting side effect of children thanking others for their help is that it tends to have a positive affect on the child's reputation. When children are dogged by problems, particularly in the case of behaviour problems, their reputation suffers and they are often criticised within their school, neighbourhood, or community. When we convert the problems into skills, and publicly talk about the skills the child is learning, it has a favourable effect on the child's reputation. A child learning a skill is not seen by the community as 'the child with those problems' but as 'the child who is learning a skill'. And this makes a big difference. When the news that the child has acquired her skill finally spreads, it has a favourable effect on the child's reputation. But her reputation fully recovers only when people hear that she has not only dealt with the problem but also has taught her new skill to someone else.

Children are natural teachers for other children

The American journalist Bob Wallace wrote this story in one of his Internet columns:

Several years ago I was bamboozled into babysitting one evening for a seven-year-old girl and two boys aged five and three. Since one of my main purposes in life is to lie on the couch and dream… I had to figure out how to get these kids to leave me alone… Plan A was to tie them up, hang them upside down in a closet and tell them they were vampire bats who had to sleep until their parents came home. I decided against this since these little potential felons might have ratted me out.

So I began to rummage around the house in the hope of discovering Plan B… a blackboard, an easel and some chalk. I set the blackboard on the easel in one of the bedrooms, sat the boys in front of it, gave the girl the chalk, and told her to teach her brothers the alphabet.

Much to my surprise, the boys sat there expectantly and the girl took on a rather 'teacherly' air. This intrigued me… The girl drew letters on the board and had her brothers repeat the names of them. She enjoyed it, and so did the monsters.

Wallace draws the conclusion that schools are 'planned wrong'. He argues that children of different ages should not be divided into different schools such as primary, secondary and high schools, but that they should all go to the same school. This would make it possible for the older children to teach the smaller ones. He speculates that if children of different age groups go to school together, the bigger ones would actively participate in teaching their juniors. This would have enormous advantages for the children's learning as well as their general development.

Children have an innate need to learn but they also have an innate need to teach. When a child teaches another child, be it his friend or sibling, he feels useful and worthwhile. If we want our children to learn things, we should see to it that they also get a chance to teach those things to others. You can imagine how encouraging it would feel for our children if, when they came home from school, we asked them, 'Who did you teach at school today?' – instead of 'What did you learn at school today?'

The circle is now almost completed. There is only one more thing to talk about: what skill will the child learn next?

Step 15

Moving on to the next skill

Find agreement with the child about the next skill to learn

Life for children is unending learning – and with everything they learn it becomes easier for them to learn more

Life is an endless learning process. When a child has acquired one skill, the next skill to be learned is already looming in sight. The idea that there are other skills to be learned after the current one is useful for both parents and children. It helps parents to be patient and to appreciate the fact that children should be allowed to concentrate on learning one skill at a time. For children it is useful because the anticipation of learning new skills increases their motivation to learn the current one.

Self-confidence

When children acquire the skills they have been learning, it gives a boost to their self-confidence and encourages them to believe in their ability to learn other skills, perhaps even more difficult ones.

The mother of seven-year-old Tim explained that Tim had been born prematurely and this had affected his development. As a result Tim had trouble learning things that required dexterity, such as buttoning clothes, drawing figures, and tying his shoelaces. The occupational therapist who was working with Tim managed to come to an agreement with him that he would start to practise the skill of tying his shoelaces. The plan worked well and with the encouragement and help of his many supporters, Tim practised persistently with the result that within two weeks he had learned the skill. When the occupational therapist met with Tim and his mother, they celebrated Tim's success. While they were drinking juice and eating buns, the occupational therapist turned to Tim and said, 'Have you decided on the next skill you want to learn?' Tim looked briefly at his mother and then explained that he had already started to learn the alphabet. His mother added that right after Tim had acquired the skill of tying his shoelaces he had started to talk about wanting to learn to read and write.

Children are proud of being allowed to move on to learning the next skill. In Keula preschool all the children have their personal posters on the wall. Looking at their posters you can see not only the skill they are currently learning but also what skills they have already learned during the current term. A long list of skills already learned is a source of pride to children – not unlike a CV or portfolio to adults in working life.

Skills in queue

Many children face not only one issue but many simultaneously. In the language of Kids' Skills we say that these children have a number of skills to learn. Since it is too difficult for most children to learn many skills at once, a child will usually be asked to concentrate on learning one skill at a time. If children have many skills to learn, it means that when one of those skills is chosen, the others will be left waiting for their turn.

Imagine a child who needs to learn to sleep in her own room, to play for some time on her own, and to brush her teeth more thoroughly. We might talk with the child and come to an agreement with her that she will start by learning to sleep in her own room. While she is learning that skill, the other two skills are waiting in a 'queue'.

When we think about skills as being in a queue, it helps us cope better with the fact that children often have several issues. We no longer see what are sometimes called 'multi-problem children', but merely children who have a number of skills to learn.

Another benefit of this skills-in-queue idea is that if new issues appear, we need not let them overwhelm us. Instead, we can think of these new issues as simply skills to be added to the queue. In the Kids' Skills Workbook there is a page reserved for writing down the skills that are waiting in a queue for the child to learn.

Children's fascination with learning yet more skills lies in the fact that getting a new skill to learn is proof they have mastered the previous skill and are considered ready to move on to the next one.

'**Now I know what skill** I want to learn next!' Carlos exclaimed to his teacher as he saw her in the morning.

'What's the hurry, young man?' said the teacher. 'You haven't even learned the one you are currently working on, have you?'

'As my next skill I want to learn to tell the truth. As soon as I have learned the skill I'm working on now I will start to learn to tell the truth,' explained Carlos.

'So you want to learn to tell the truth?' wondered the teacher aloud. 'That's a fine thing to learn but why on earth do you need to learn to do that? You're not in the habit of telling stories. At least I've never noticed you doing that.'

Carlos explained. 'I lied to my mum and now I want to learn to tell her the truth. Yesterday Mum was home and I played with my friends in the street in front of the house where we live. Mum told me to stay there and not to go anywhere but I went with my friends to a park in our neighbourhood. Later when I went home, Mum said that she had been looking for me all over the place and that she hadn't found me anywhere in the street. I told her I'd been in the street all the time and she just hadn't seen me. She said it was a shame that I hadn't kept my promise and stayed in the street, because if I'd been there she would have taken me to the amusement park. She also said that she can't take me to the amusement park until I learn to tell the truth!'

We have now familiarised ourselves with the fifteen steps of Kids' Skills and have a relatively good grasp of the central ideas of the method. Let's now go on and take a closer look at how to apply these ideas when dealing with some common issues for children.

Finding solutions with the help of Kids' Skills

Kids' Skills can be used for helping children deal with a wide variety of problems: behavioural issues, bad habits, fears, learning difficulties, and issues related to bodily functions such as speaking, sleeping, eating, urinating and defecating. In addition to psychological issues, Kids' Skills can also be used as an adjunct in the rehabilitation of children experiencing problems with a neurological basis.

In this section we will look at how to use Kids' Skills in helping children find solutions to some common (and less common) problems.

The majority of the examples in this section have been provided by people around the world who use Kids' Skills – either with the children they work with or while raising their own children.

At Helsinki Brief Therapy Institute we collect stories about experiences of using Kids' Skills from around the world. The archives are used for the purpose of research and refining the method. Please feel free to contribute to this archive by sending your own Kids' Skills story to Helsinki Brief Therapy Institute, Haapalahdenkatu 1,00300 Helsinki, or by email to feedback@kidsskills.org.

Bad habits

At some point during their development most children exhibit some kind of undesirable repetitive behaviour. Common examples of such behaviour include nail biting, thumb sucking and hair twisting. Children can also have many kinds of peculiar eating or sleeping habits and tics (sudden involuntary movements in the area of the eyes or mouth).

If you have ever had a 'bad habit' of any kind you know how difficult it is to get rid of it. Many of us with bad habits have tried to promise ourselves 'never to do it again' – only to catch ourselves just minutes later doing the exact same thing.

You may also have noticed that attempts to help other people get rid of their bad habits often fail. It is also not uncommon that attempts to influence other people's bad habits backfire, only causing an increase in the frequency of the habit.

It is therefore of great importance to know how to help our children overcome their unhelpful repetitive behaviours. We have found that it is better to help children replace their bad habits with other, less disturbing, habits, than to try to help them get rid of the bad ones. As the saying goes, 'It's easier to start something new than to stop something old.'

Before children can learn to replace their unwanted habits with better habits, they need to learn to become aware of the times when the bad habit occurs. Only when the child has become aware of 'doing' his habit can he learn to replace it with another one.

When twelve-year-old Lisa was to quit biting her nails, she first needed to learn to notice when she was doing it, or even better, when she was about to do it. This awareness would allow her to consciously replace her biting habit with an alternative. Lisa herself came up with the idea that whenever she noticed that she was biting her nails, or about to bite them, she would do something else with her fingers. She suggested that she start to carry a nail file with her at all times so that she could use it to take care of her nails instead of using her teeth for the same purpose. In order to remember to do that, she even came up with the clever idea that she hang a file around her neck for it to be always available.

Four-year-old Jeremy had the habit of sucking his thumb. 'Next time you get the urge to suck your thumb again, what could you do instead?' his mother asked him. Jeremy thought for a few seconds, then folded his thumb with the fingers of the other hand and said, 'I could do this. I could squeeze my thumb with the fingers of my other hand like this.'

Alan had the bad habit of using four-letter words. His father had tried both punishment and reward to make him stop but with no success. One day Alan's father came up with the idea of replacing bad habits with better habits. He immediately went over to Alan and explained that he wanted Alan to learn the art of replacing all four-letter words with more suitable alternatives. Alan was to learn to say, for example, 'give me a break', instead of 'f--k you', or 'get out of here' instead of 'f--k off'.

Alan didn't know what benefit learning such a silly skill would have for him, or anyone else, for that matter. However, after his father had had a serious discussion with him about the issue, he began to understand that the skill of replacing swearwords with more suitable expressions was indeed a useful skill to have. He understood that his constant swearing could give people the impression that this was the way his father spoke to him at home, too. That was not true, and Alan didn't want people to think that it was. His father also managed to help Alan understand that many children shy away from kids who swear all the time. The father succeeded in convincing Alan that for a child to become popular among friends, it is actually of more use to steer clear of swearing.

Together father and son designed a playful game to practise replacing four-letter words with acceptable words. They made a list of all the swearwords that Alan was currently using, and then agreed on the expression with which they would be replaced.

Having done that, they started practising this replacing skill that is so important for children to learn. They did it by talking casually about this and that, and whenever Alan was about to spit out a swearword they would use the replacement expression instead.

Alan called the skill he was learning 'well-mannered speaking' and together with his father he told a number of people about his project. The list of swearwords and their corresponding replacement expressions was placed on the wall of Alan's room, where it created interest among his friends.

Alan and his father told Alan's teacher about the project. They also agreed with the teacher that if Alan sometimes forgot to replace a four-letter word with an acceptable expression, the teacher would point her index finger at Alan as an indication that he needed to guard his tongue and quickly replace the swearword with an acceptable expression. Alan practised his skill industriously and even if he did forget it once in a while he made rapid progress. His supporters noticed it and were generous in giving him positive feedback. Even his older brother, who was quite tired of Alan's constant swearing, acknowledged his progress. After five weeks his father agreed that Alan had learned, reasonably well, to guard his tongue, so he arranged a celebration where pancakes and hot chocolate were served.

It is not easy to rid oneself of bad habits, especially when those habits have become ingrained. Yet it is possible, particularly if we don't try to get rid of the bad habit directly but learn to replace it with a better habit instead. And to do that, we obviously need to practise, to perform the better habit again and again until it comes to us just as naturally as the old one. Once that starts to happen, we realise that in fact we can have more control over our bad habits than we previously thought we could.

Speaking of bad habits, I am reminded of an eight-year-old boy whose mother contacted me because of his peculiar habit of eating thread. He would pull thread from his clothes and eat metres of it, destroying practically all his clothes. I gave the mother instructions about how she could teach her son to replace his bad habit with a better one. The mother understood my instructions and tried the approach. She taught him to play with a piece of thread without ingesting it but the system only worked when she was around. The moment the mother disappeared from his sight the boy would start ingesting thread again.

Finally, after some months, the mother called me again and told me that the boy had had a check-up at the health care clinic. Some basic laboratory tests had been done and it was found that he was suffering from a relatively severe case of anaemia. The doctor had prescribed iron supplement medication and within just a few days of taking the medication his thread eating had totally ceased.

Obviously most bad habits are not caused by a dietary lack, but the story teaches us the important lesson that we should always keep our eyes open; peculiar behaviour may sometimes have a physiological rather than a psychological basis.

Aggressive behaviour

Many children sometimes behave violently towards other children or even towards their own parents. When these children become angry, for whatever reason, they react by biting, hitting, kicking or shoving whoever comes their way. According to the Kids' Skills philosophy, aggressive behaviour can be seen as a symptom of a lack of a basic skill that all children need in order not to revert to aggressive behaviour towards other people. For example, if a child hits other children who refuse to give her the toys she wants, we can say that this child lacks some skill that all children need to be able to deal with such situations more constructively. The skill this child would need might be, for example, the ability to take no for an answer, or the ability to persuade other children to voluntarily give her the toys that she wants from them.

When children behave aggressively it is not always clear what skill they are lacking. One could argue that all aggressive children are lacking the skill of self-control or the skill of managing their anger, but according to Kids' Skills such skills are 'big' or complex skills that need to be divided into smaller skills before it is possible for the child to learn them.

Mat, Ashley, Elena and Sean all share the same behaviour: they all behave aggressively towards other people. But even if on the surface they all seem to have the same behaviour, a closer look reveals that each of them is lacking a different skill.

Mat's violent behaviour occurs in situations where other children come near him – when they, as Mat sees it, violate his territory. For Mat to overcome his violent behaviour he needs to learn to become comfortable with the physical proximity of other children.

Ashley's violent behaviour occurs in situations where he feels that another child is teasing him or getting on his nerves. For him to overcome his violence he needs to learn to deal with those situations in a better way. He may, for example, need to learn to go and tell the teacher what has happened instead of hitting other children.

Elena's violent behaviour occurs in situations when she is denied something she desperately wants. In those situations she may begin to scratch or kick the person who refuses to yield to her. For Helen to overcome her violence, she needs to learn to deal more constructively with frustrations or situations in which she does not get her way.

Sean's violence appears to be nothing but a bad habit. Whenever he gets mad, for whatever reason, he is likely to bite whoever happens to be next to him at that moment. The best way for Sean to overcome his violence would probably be that he learns to replace his bad habit with a better habit – such as biting his sleeve instead of biting people.

According to this logic, violent behaviour is caused by a lack of skills, but what these missing skills might be varies from child to child. We may, however, identify the missing skill by analysing the situations in which the child behaves violently. When we have an idea about which skill the child is missing, it is easier for us to help the child overcome his violent behaviour.

One might even say that there are no violent children, only children who tend to behave violently in certain situations because they lack specific skills they need to behave in a more constructive way.

Viveka Liljeros, a school counsellor from Sweden, has told the following story:

Stefan was seven years old and was attending first class in school. He got into fights with other children at every single break and all the other children were afraid of him. I received an invitation from the headmaster to come to a meeting at the school where Stefan's issues were to be discussed.

'Will Stefan himself be present?' I asked the headmaster.

'That is not the plan, but both of his parents are coming as well as his teacher and the school nurse,' he said.

Inspired by Kids' Skills, I suggested that we ask Stefan to join us. The headmaster accepted my suggestion and the next day we all sat in the meeting talking about Stefan's situation.

The meeting started with the headmaster introducing everyone present. Stefan swung his legs nervously and the mood was tense. When the teacher was about to begin telling us about Stefan's behaviour, I asked to speak. 'Before we start to speak about your fighting, Stefan, I'd like to know what you are good at? What can you do well?'

I found out that Stefan was good at maths. In fact he was so good that he had worked his way through his maths book, all on his own, several pages ahead of what the other children were learning. It also became evident that Stefan had a talent for drawing. When I heard about it, I asked to see a sample. Stefan quickly drew a fun picture that was passed around the room for everyone to admire.

'What do you like to do with your friends?' I asked him next, and he told me about football and other games he liked.

Out of the corner of my eye I thought I saw the headmaster and the teacher becoming impatient. After all, we had come together to talk about the problems involving Stefan, not about his hobbies and the things he was good at. It was time to talk business.

'I have heard that things don't always work that well between you and your friends. Is that so?'

'It is,' answered Stefan.

'So what is it that happens during breaks?'

'I get into fights because I hit others when I get mad at them.'

'In that case I think I can understand you, because usually bad things happen when you hit others. But tell me what it is that you need to learn to do so that you don't hit others.'

'I need to learn to control myself and keep my hands crossed behind my back.'

I couldn't believe my ears. He spoke as if he too had taken a course in Kids' Skills.

'I bet it's not that easy to control yourself and to keep your hands crossed behind your back when you become angry. Would you like your teacher and your friends to help you remember to do that?'

Stefan nodded in agreement.

'How would you want them to do that?'

Stefan thought for a while but couldn't come up with an answer.

'I have a suggestion for you,' I said. 'From tomorrow on, you start practising controlling yourself during recess by keeping your hands behind your back. Then every day, at the end of the day, you get together with your teacher briefly to talk about the day. If you succeeded in keeping your hands behind your back that day you will talk about how you did it. If you didn't succeed, you will talk about what to do to succeed the next day. What do you think?'

Stefan liked the idea and the teacher too nodded carefully. I also made the suggestion that the teacher give Stefan some kind of mark for every recess that had worked well.

'Let's say you are able to avoid fights every single recess for three weeks in a row, what would you want to have as a reward?'

'A Kinder-egg!' said Stefan with delight in his voice. A Kinder-egg is a chocolate egg available in European shops during Easter.

'Sounds good to me,' I said. 'I can come back to the school after two weeks and then I'll come to meet you. Then I will find out how you have done. Can we shake hands on this deal?'

Stefan shook hands with all of us and we ended the meeting. After the meeting I stayed for a while to talk with the teacher. She said that she would go along with the plan but that she was doubtful it would work. I promised to call the school the next day to find out how things were going with Stefan.

When I called the school next day the teacher answered in a cheerful voice and said that Stefan had behaved like an angel. He had got two big marks in his notebook and everyone had wondered about his improved behaviour. Two weeks later, when I was at the school again, I learned that the teacher had indeed had a brief meeting every day with Stefan and that he had got a mark of up to 95 per cent at each recess. When there had been recesses where things had not worked that well, Stefan had talked with the teacher – not about what went wrong but specifically about what to do during the next recess to get back on track. The teacher had also found out that the fights during the breaks were not all caused by Stefan and that certain boys had got into the habit of deliberately provoking him.

I also happened to bump into Stefan in the hallway. He came running to me with a cheerful face.

'Hey Stefan, now you can tell me how you've been doing.'

'I've been doing really well,' Stefan answered proudly.

'That's great! How on earth have you been able to succeed that well?'

'I've controlled myself and kept my hands behind my back,' he explained. He then gave me an example of a situation where a girl had bitten his arm and he had done nothing. He had just left the situation. He also said that it had been helpful to talk to the teacher every day. I suggested to Stefan that he should get a certificate for having learned to control himself so well but he didn't like the idea at all. Instead he wanted the Kinder-egg, which he eventually got.

Lisa Brennan, a consultant at a child psychiatric outpatient service in Dublin, has told the following story:

Six-year-old Mark was referred to our service by his mother on the advice of his teacher four weeks after starting primary school, because of severe behaviour problems in school and at home. Mark had already been assessed by a social worker, a child psychiatrist and child-care worker and he had a two-year history of a series of interventions, including behaviour modification, parenting input, group work and school-based intervention, with little success. According to the child psychiatrist his behaviours fitted the criteria of what is called 'oppositional defiant disorder'.

Mark's parents and teachers agreed that his three main issues were wandering around the classroom, speaking out when others were speaking, and acting in a rough and aggressive manner with other children. These problem behaviours were causing severe difficulty in the school setting and with peer interaction, and were causing problems at home too. Mark's target skills were identified as:

- learning to sit on his chair in class
- learning to listen when others were speaking
- learning to play gently with peers.

Mark decided to start with the skill of playing gently with peers. This was the most urgent to him as the school had suggested that he only be allowed out to the schoolyard if supervised by his parents. Mark's parents spoke of the burden of constantly being called to see the teacher after school. The parents all wait together to collect their children and being called out to speak to the teacher was described by Mark's mother as 'doing the walk of shame'.

Mark saw two main benefits of learning the skill: his parents would not be asked to supervise him in the playground and he might be invited to other children's parties if their parents did not see him as 'rough'. This was important information for Mark's parents as they had been unaware of his sense of exclusion from the other children's parties.

Mark had no problem finding a name for his skill. He named it 'play easy'. This is a frequently used local term to describe playing quietly and in a trouble-free manner. When asked to choose a power creature, Mark chose Batman. He had a picture of Batman in his schoolbag as well as in his Kids' Skills workbook, and in addition he carried a small Batman figure in his pocket for school. As the primary issue was school based, it was felt to be important that Mark had his power creature available to him not only in class but also in the yard.

Mark and his parents enjoyed all this very much. Mark said it would be good to be telling his family and friends something good about himself instead of always telling them he'd been in trouble. Skill learning was a source of pride for Mark.

To build Mark's confidence his parents spoke to him about all the skills he already had and about the times in the past when he was able to 'play easy'. Mark's own comment was: 'It's easy to learn things but very hard to be good at them.'

When asked about how he wanted to celebrate in the end, Mark said he wanted to visit the wax museum because there was a large wax figure of Batman there. He planned the trip to the wax museum together with his parents and the idea was that he would go there together with his two cousins and three of his schoolmates. This type of trip had never been possible before because Mark's behaviour could not be trusted in these types of situations. There was a clear consensus that the celebration would only occur when Mark had demonstrated his skill at home – and at school in most of his interactions with other children – for four weeks in a row.

The most interesting step of Kids' Skills, for both Mark and his family, came when Mark was to demonstrate his skill. Mark's dad undertook to role-play interactions with Mark to enable him to perform the skill. This was important not only to Mark but also to his father, because it allowed him to be useful to his son and to feel that he could help him in a practical way. It helped the father become empowered and confident as a parent. A great side effect!

The idea of going public was not in any way difficult for Mark or his family as everyone felt that the problems were already public property. Mark's parents felt that going public would demonstrate to family and friends that they were trying to help their son to resolve his difficulties.

Mark and his parents were told about setbacks and had it explained that this was something to be expected. They were introduced to the idea that sometimes power creatures are so busy that they leave children on their own even before the child they are helping has gained full mastery of his skill. Mark was impressed by this idea. He said, 'So if I make a mistake, you won't all give up on me.'

I tried to think of ways in which Mark could have taught his 'play easy' skill to other children but didn't come up with any good ideas. On review, however, Mark's parents were proud to report that Mark had been overheard teaching his three-year-old cousin how to play easy. This passing the skill on to someone else had occurred at his own pace without adult suggestion or encouragement.

Five weeks after the initial introduction to Kids' Skills, Mark had his celebration. He had a good report from school. Local mothers had commented on the improvement in his behaviour with peers, and local children were calling to play with him. Mark used his celebration to thank his supporters. When asked what skill he wanted to learn next, Mark said he had decided to work on sitting in his chair.

Mark and his parents found the process positive whereas previous interventions had left them feeling distressed and helpless.

Depression, loss and grief

When dealing with unhappy children, or children suffering from depression, professionals these days tend to say you should try to remove the cause of their unhappiness. This, however, is not always possible, and in such cases it may be wise to focus on the future and try to find out what the child needs to learn to be able to retrieve her happiness.

Different unhappy children need to learn different things to rediscover happiness, but generally speaking one could say that unhappy children need to learn to become better at enjoying life. In other words they need to retrieve the joy they have lost.

Tapani Ahola, my long-time colleague, has told the following story:

Larry was a twelve-year-old boy who was depressed. His mother had died of cancer two years earlier and soon thereafter Larry had begun to suffer from depression and anxiety. Larry lived with his father. After his mother's death Larry had given up his hobbies and begun to avoid the company of his friends. About the only pastime he had was to sit in front of the TV with his father and eat. Not surprisingly both father and son were considerably overweight.

Larry was referred for consultation to the child guidance centre by the school. His depression and anxiety had gradually become worse, to the point that for the past month he had not even had the energy to attend school.

We briefly discussed the tragedy this family had encountered and talked for a while about Larry's unhappiness. I then raised the question of what Larry needed to learn so that he could get back to school and overcome his unhappiness and anxiety. The conclusion was that Larry needed to reclaim his initiative and his ability to enjoy life. He named this new project of his 'happy again'.

When it was time to think about how Larry could practise becoming 'happy again', I asked him and his father what enjoyable things they had done together in the past. This led to a discussion which revealed that because of Larry's depression and anxiety, father and son had done none of the enjoyable things they used to do when Larry's mother was still alive. In fact, in the past they had had many mutual hobbies. Among other things they used to go on fishing trips, they went together to swim at the local pool, and in the winter they went snowboarding together.

I made the suggestion that they pick up their old hobbies again and start to do the enjoyable things they used to do together before Larry's mother died. After a brief negotiation both Larry and his father went along with the plan.

During the following weeks Larry and his father did as we had decided. They began to do again the very same things that had previously brought joy to Larry's life. After just a couple of weeks Larry was back to school. In a couple of months he had gone down three kilos in weight, and he had many funny stories about what he had done with his dad.

Fears and nightmares

Let's imagine a girl – we will call her Anna – who is so afraid of the bogeyman that she does not dare sleep in her own room. When she sleeps in her parents' room she disturbs their sleep. Her parents want her to learn to sleep in her own room, but for her to be able to do that she needs to overcome her fear of 'the bogey'.

How could Anna overcome her fear of bogeys with the help of Kids' Skills? What skill should she master to conquer her fear? Should she learn to understand that bogeys are not real – that they don't even exist – or should she rather learn to come to terms with them, so as to realise that she doesn't have to be afraid of them? The latter alternative is more appealing because all parents know that explaining to a child afraid of bogeys that there are no such things does not do the trick. After all, why would a child who has seen bogeys under her bed with her own eyes believe anybody telling her that they don't exist?

Let's imagine that we ask Anna how she would teach another child to overcome an unnecessary fear.

'You know, Anna, there are some children who are afraid of having their hair cut. Some of these children are so afraid of having their hair cut that they refuse to let anybody cut their hair even when they really need a haircut. How would you, Anna, teach a child afraid of having a haircut that there is nothing to be afraid of?'

Anna might answer: 'I would tell that child that it doesn't hurt and that she has nothing to be afraid of.'

'That's a good idea,' we would say to Anna, 'but what if that child would not take your word for it? How would you help her become convinced that there's really nothing to be afraid of when having a haircut?'

Anna might say: 'I would take a pair of scissors in my hand and I would let her cut some of my hair first. Then I would cut some of her hair so that she would see that it doesn't hurt and that there is nothing to be afraid of.'

See? Children know that to overcome fears you need to conquer them.

They understand that you don't overcome a fear by hearing adults, or other children, tell you that there is nothing to be afraid of. Instead, children conquer fears by making closer contact with what they are afraid of until they learn from their own experience that they don't need to be afraid any more.

When we use Kids' Skills to help children overcome fears we do it by encouraging children to become familiar with the thing they are afraid of.

Sam was a boy of five who didn't want to leave his home because of an intense fear of dogs. His parents knew that Sam would overcome his fear of dogs if only he could stay for a longer time close to a dog. In other words, if there were a way to get Sam to become used to dogs, he would probably overcome his phobia.

Sam's parents came up with the following idea. They explained to Sam that in one of the kennels in town there was a puppy with a big problem. The puppy's problem was that it was afraid of humans. For that puppy to overcome its fear of humans it needed to be adopted by a human who would teach the dog that there was no need to be afraid. Together with his parents Sam went to the kennel and picked up the puppy that was afraid of humans. As the puppy matured, it learned that there was not really any need to be afraid of people. Meanwhile Sam also learned that dogs make good play companions.

We can apply the same principle to children who are afraid of monsters, bogeys, or any other scary imaginary beings. As children become acquainted with what they are afraid of, they learn – through their own experience – that there is nothing to fear. It is a positive experience for children to find out that what they thought were scary monsters are in fact benevolent beings such as fairies or elves guarding their sleep.

The best way for children to overcome phobias is to develop a particular courage that drains the phobia. It is easier for children to learn or to develop courage than to try to overcome a phobia. Developing courage means that you become so familiar with what you fear that you are no longer afraid of it. Courage is like a skill. It too can be learned through practice.

Hooshmand Ebrahimi, a child counsellor from Iran, has told the following story:

Ali was ten years old and he suffered from nightmares in which he was being chased. My colleague examined the boy carefully and found nothing physically wrong with him that might have explained his nightmares. I then had a discussion with Ali's parents and came to the conclusion with them that for their son to overcome his nightmares, he would need to learn to change his dreams so that they would have a happy ending instead of a gloomy one. We agreed that the parents would continue to comfort Ali at night if he woke up to a nightmare. That would help him calm down while he was learning to convert nightmares into 'goodmares'.

Having spoken with Ali's parents, I talked with him alone. I told him that he needed to learn the skill of converting his nightmares into 'goodmares' and he agreed with me. I asked him what good it would do him to learn to be able to do that. He answered that if he learned that skill he would be able to sleep in his own bed and to be in the dark. He also thought that having that skill would make him healthier and help him get better grades at school. Our discussion about the benefits of knowing how to convert nightmares into 'goodmares' increased his motivation to do something to learn the skill.

Ali named his skill 'the happy sleeper'. Here in Iran children have a TV program with a comic puppet by the same name that falls asleep all over the place. As his power creature Ali chose Rostam, who was supposed to protect him from the persecutors in his dreams. Rostam is an important and well-known mythical hero in Persian folklore, much like Hercules in the Western world. As his supporters, Ali picked his parents, his best friend and his football coach.

Our search for reasons to believe that Ali would be able to learn the 'happy sleeper' skill yielded the following arguments:

• Ali wanted to learn the skill.

• He had chosen the art and drama group as an extracurricular activity.

• Ali's football coach believed that he would learn because he had learned even more difficult things that had to do with football.

Then it was time to think about how to celebrate when Ali had learned his skill. Ali wanted to invite his friends to a party where they would eat football-shaped pasta, which is actually available in our country.

'Think about the time when you have learned to make bad dreams into pleasant dreams,' I asked Ali. 'What will you do then if you happen to have a bad dream?' Ali described one of his nightmares and then started to write a happy ending for the dream. Rostam, the hero of heroes, was the protector of Ali in his new dream ending. Having explained the new dream to me, Ali also acted for me what he had imagined. I encouraged Ali to repeat his bad dream and to imagine various good endings to it. The rehearsal helped Ali to achieve a sense of mastery.

It was a good thing that Ali informed all his supporters about what he was up to. For this purpose he prepared a poster with his name, a picture of Rostam and the name of his skill. The poster was placed on the wall of his room for his supporters to see. His supporters played an important role. They asked him to show them his skill and then admired him when he did it.

Before arranging the celebration, I brought up the possibility that some time in the future Ali might have a bad dream again. I explained to him that this could happen when Rostam decided to leave him to go to protect other children. We then made plans about how to deal with such a situation and came to an agreement that whenever Ali had a bad dream again he would call Rostam to get back his feeling of power.

At the celebration, Ali expressed thanks to his supporters and once again demonstrated his skill of turning an unpleasant dream into a pleasant one. One of his classmates asked him, 'How can I get rid of a dream in which I am falling?' Ali explained to him, 'First of all you need to have a power creature like Rostam. It will give you the strength you need to overcome your falling dream.' Then Ali went on to explain to his classmate how to use drawing to imagine another ending to the dream.

Ali had not only learned the skill of having pleasant dreams. He had even taught it to another child.

Behavioural problems

One of the most common issues in schools and day care facilities today is rough social behaviour, or a lack of social skills. Children for whom this is an issue need to become better at playing and interacting with other children and adults. In fact, in most schools and child care facilities nowadays, social skills are at the top of the list of educational goals. Children learn social skills as part of their curriculum but many children also need a personal social skills training program. This is where Kids' Skills can come in handy.

Alfred Bratteru, who works as an instructor at an afternoon care centre for schoolchildren in Oslo, Norway, has told the following story:

Anders was a hyperactive boy who was so quick to go into rage that none of the other children wanted to play with him. I sat down with my colleague to think about what skill Anders would need to learn. We came to the conclusion that he needed to learn to talk and to behave calmly. I went to Anders and told him what we thought he needed to learn. He fully agreed with me. I asked Anders who he wanted to ask to become his secret supporters. He mentioned the names of four of the other boys of his own age who also attended our centre.

The next day I went over to the four boys that Anders had pointed out to ask them if they would like to become Anders' supporters. To my surprise, I learned from them that Anders had already asked them the day before and that they had agreed. It seemed to me that they were downright proud of being Anders' secret supporters. In fact the boys had already started to come up with plans about how to help Anders learn to become calmer.

After a couple of days one of Anders' supporters came over and whispered to me that they – all five boys together – had started to practise calm behaviour. He pointed out that this was a secret that should not be revealed to anyone. In other words, we had at our afternoon centre a team of five boys secretly practising calm behaviour.

One day soon after, Anders ran to me and told me proudly, 'Now I know it works!'

'What works, Anders?' I asked him.

'When I calmly asked the graduates for "*russ-cards*", I got loads of them. See for yourself!' And at that Anders, with a radiating face, reached into his pocket and produced a pile of no less than 73 russ-cards.

Russ-cards, by the way, are part of a Norwegian tradition. Every year, in May, when high school students stop going to school, there is a big and loud celebration during which the students give out cards that bear some resemblance to business cards. In addition to the name and a picture of the student, there is always something witty written on the card, usually something with a double meaning. The students drive around the town in large, colourfully painted trucks giving out their cards to each other as well as to younger schoolchildren who would do anything to collect as many of them as possible.

In fact the students are usually annoyed by the large number of noisy children screaming for their cards. Anders was wise to take another approach. He asked for the cards calmly instead of shouting and screaming like others. He had succeeded in taking his skill to the real world outside the boundaries of our afternoon centre and realised that learning the skill actually paid off.

This was the first time in his seven years of life that Anders had friends of his own age who sincerely wanted him to succeed and who were willing to do anything to help him acquire the skills he needed. Together these boys had worked out a number of secret signs and they had planned how to make his life better and easier. No wonder Anders was radiating.

It's now more than a year since we started using Kids' Skills with Anders and he is now in the second grade. He is a calm boy these days and we have heard from his teacher that he is doing well at school.

Rituals

It is not uncommon for children around ten to present with various kinds of ritualistic behaviours – forms of obsession or compulsion. These are repetitive actions, or thoughts, that the child feels an urge to perform over and over again, and always in the same way. If we try to prevent children from acting out their rituals they tend to become anxious, and often go into a rage. There are many kinds of rituals. Here are a few examples:

- Tina brushes her teeth at least ten times every evening. She cannot explain her behaviour in any way other than by saying that she has the feeling her teeth are not clean.

- Jack touches objects three, five or seven times. He has a superstitious belief that if he doesn't do it something bad will happen to his parents or to someone else he cares for.

- Beth performs a compulsive ritual in which she has to arrange her dolls, her teddy bears and her pillows into a precise order, and when she is done she starts to flatten out every fold in her blanket. The ritual takes more than an hour of her time every evening.

- Mike collects bottle tops. Always when he is walking outside he keeps his eyes on the ground and when he spots a bottle top he just has to pick it up to include it in his collection.

We can help children overcome obsessive rituals with Kids' Skills, but to do that we first have to establish what skill the child needs to practise so that the ritual can be left behind.

A mother from Finland provided the following story:

When Kim was twelve, she suffered from many different rituals. Among other things she always touched door handles twice, and in the evenings she went through her school bag over and over again to make sure nothing was missing. She also collected sweet wrappings and rubbed them meticulously to smooth them out. If I even dared to suggest throwing the sweet wrapping away, she became furious. When she walked outside she was always careful not to step on any cracks or seams in the pavement.

Many of Kim's rituals were harmless but one of them was particularly annoying: every evening before going to bed Kim had to arrange all the things in her sight and place them in a particular way. This ritual had become so bad that it could take her up to two hours. Kim was even afraid of going to bed because she knew that as soon as she lay her head on her pillow she would get the urge to arrange things to place them 'right'.

Kim usually didn't like talking about her rituals, but she once told me that she just had to arrange the things correctly because she was afraid that something bad would happen to me or to her father. When I asked her what bad thing she was afraid would happen to us, she said that we might die. This was a peculiar way of thinking but it was very real for her.

I tried to get advice from all the child experts I knew but no one was able to tell me anything that would have been useful. I told my husband about Kids' Skills and together we decided to try it with Kim. We explained to her that the skill we wanted her to learn was for her to be able to go to sleep with a feeling of security. She agreed with us. We then continued to explain that for her to learn that she needed to develop an ability to disregard whatever dreadful thoughts might enter her mind. Kim still agreed with us. When I asked her to give a name to that skill, she couldn't think of anything. Together we talked about a 'silly thoughts terminator', and then came up with 'the silly nilly skill'.

The most difficult part of the process was to come up with a way for Kim to practise her skill. Finally we invented an exercise, which turned out to be quite funny. It consisted of a game we played with her in the evening at the time she was going to bed. One of us would go to her room and sit by her bed. Then we would tell her all kinds of superstitious thoughts similar to those she had the habit of creating in her own head. She was to respond to what we had said by saying 'Silly nilly!' and by demonstrating with her facial expressions that she was able to pay no attention to our sinister predictions.

For example, I might have said to her: 'If you do not knock the table three times with your nose, our dog will be run over by a car tomorrow and die.' 'Silly nilly,' Kim said, while showing with her facial expression that she didn't believe such a superstitious claim.

Here are some more examples of lines we used:

- 'If you don't kiss both of your hands twice now, there will a thunderstorm in the night and it will blow away the roof of our house!'

- 'If you don't move that pillow to a better position, Dad's car won't start in the morning.'

- 'If you don't think a kind thought right now, your sister will step on a banana peel tomorrow and fall and dislocate her nose.'

This may sound silly, but this was the only way we could exercise her ability to disregard or ignore the superstitious thoughts that her mind produced. For the first week we trained with Kim every evening but after that we simply forgot about it because of Kim's rapid progress. I can still sometimes catch her paying a bit too much attention to how she places the pillows on her bed but it's two years since we did the 'anti-superstition training' with her and I think it is safe to say that the anxiety and the annoying rituals belong to the past.

One of the most common obsessive-compulsive behaviours in children is excessive anxiousness – a tendency to constantly worry that something terrible is going to happen. In child psychiatry this problem is called 'overanxious disorder of childhood'. The following story is from a mother who helped her son beat his habit of worrying excessively about everything.

Tom was nine years old, and he was worried about everything. I mean it, about everything. He was afraid that something bad would happen to me, that he would get lost, that there would be a catastrophe, that a war would break out, that terrorists would attack – you name it. Because of his worries Tom could not be alone for one minute. At night he had trouble falling asleep, and at school, according to his teacher, he always sat in class with an anxious look on his face.

I heard about Kids' Skills, and when I came home that day I said to Tom that I would need to talk with him later because there was a new skill he needed to learn. Tom was enthusiastic and he wanted to know immediately what the skill was. I told him that we would talk about it in the evening and then sent him out to play with his friends.

In the evening when we sat down for supper I told Tom that I had learned that all the problems children have only happen because children have not learned some important skill. I explained to him that he too could become free of his fears and worries if only he learned the right skill. We thought together about what skill he needed to learn and came to the conclusion that he needed the skill of throwing worries away. When I asked him what he wanted to call this skill he immediately had the answer. The skill was to be called 'Mister Bean'.

We then started to think about what good it would do him if he learned the 'Mister Bean' skill. Tom said that life would be easier for him. I suggested that if he had that skill he would be left with a lot more time to spend with his friends. Tom accepted this and added that he would be happier if he didn't have so many things to worry about all the time.

Then it was time to choose a power creature. Tom didn't hesitate on this one, either. He wanted his power creature to be the computer game hero Super Mario. From the instruction booklet that came with the game we found a picture of Super Mario, which we cut out and glued to the cover of Tom's Kids' Skills workbook. When I asked Tom in what way he thought that Super Mario would help him learn the Mister Bean skill, he said without giving it any further thought: 'It will kick and hit the worries away and it will suffocate any worry by throwing coins at them.'

The most difficult part of the process was for us to convince Tom that he would be able to learn the skill. Perhaps it was more my problem since it wasn't easy for me to convince myself that he would learn the Mister Bean skill, particularly because I knew how difficult giving up worries was for him. Finding supporters, instead, was both easy and fun. As Tom's group of supporters grew bigger, he also gained more confidence. With many supporters he no longer needed to feel he was struggling with his anxiety all by himself. We even tried to make some plans about the party but at that point Tom became tired and asked me if we could continue with Kids' Skills another day.

The next morning when Tom was at the door leaving to catch the school bus, he once again said those very same words he always said to me when he was leaving for school: 'Take care, Mum, and promise not to hurt yourself.' This time I didn't even try to convince him that he had nothing to worry about. I just winked and said, smiling, 'Mister Bean.' Tom laughed.

At school Tom told his teacher that he was practising the Mister Bean skill and showed her his Kids' Skills workbook. The teacher looked at it carefully and said to Tom that it was good for him to learn the Mister Bean skill.

We found a way for Tom to practise throwing away worries. In this game I came up with all kinds of funny worries and said them aloud. I said, for example, 'Let's hope our house has not caught fire while we have been away', or 'Let's hope there won't be the thunderstorm of the century that will leave us without electricity for a long time.' When I had said something like that Tom was supposed to demonstrate that he was able to not become worried. In addition to the worries that I came up with, Tom still had lots of worries of his own. Whenever he brought up his own worries I reminded him of his skill by saying to him either 'Mister Bean' or 'Super Mario'. Those were the magic words with the help of which Tom was able to throw away his worries and to convince himself that there really wasn't anything to worry about.

Tom's worrying had been a serious problem for us because it prevented him from doing any new things, such as taking up new hobbies, or going to camps. When I realised that Tom was making progress, I got the courage to enrol him for a camp, which was due the next summer. But in the spring, as the day approached for Tom to stay at the camp site for a week to meet up with all the other children who were going to the summer camp, he began to come up with all kinds of excuses to avoid going.

I took Tom on my lap and explained to him that we had been practising the Mister Bean skill to overcome these kinds of situations and that this visit to the summer camp place was an opportunity for him to see how much he had learned. I assured him that there was nothing for him to worry about and that the visit would be an opportunity for him to decide whether he wanted to go to summer camp for two weeks or not. Tom agreed to go. I must admit that at this stage I was still thinking that in the summer he would refuse to go and would want to stay home with me all summer long.

But the week at the camp went so well that when Tom returned he immediately announced that he wanted to go there in the summer. At that point it was easy for me to praise him for the progress he had made.

We have benefited from Kids' Skills in many ways. The practising of throwing away worries has made me realise the magnitude of worries that poor Tom had been carrying on his shoulders. Sometimes Tom has even spotted me worrying about something in vain. In those situations he has said to me, 'You know, Mum, you too need some Mister Bean practice.' Kids' Skills has also helped us talk about things that are not easy to talk about. For example, on the few occasions when I have snapped at Tom with irritation in my voice, he has said to me, 'You need to practise talking kindly so you don't get nervous so easily.'

Last summer Tom went, for the first time in his life, on a summer camp and everything went well. One day at the end of the summer, Tom came home with his best friend, Arnold, and asked me to come to talk with them. Gradually it dawned on me what this was all about. Arnold had told Tom about some problem of his and Tom had told him about Kids' Skills. Together the two boys had come to the conclusion that for Arnold to get free of the problem, he needed to learn a skill that was given the name of 'the howdy skill'. But how Arnold learned his 'howdy' skill is another story.

Bullying

Bullying is common among children. The usual (and often the best) way to intervene when bullying occurs is to get the children together and help them find a solution themselves. Sometimes, however, this course of action does not work. In such cases we can consider the alternative of helping the child who is being bullied to become more resilient.

Ron was a thirteen-year-old boy who was bullied for having a cleft palate (a congenital malformation of the area of the mouth and nose). Even though Ron had been operated on quite a few times, the sound of his voice was still somewhat nasal and his nose was slightly tilted to the side. His face was to some extent disfigured.

The issue, for his parents as well as for Ron, was that Ron didn't go anywhere. His mother had tried everything to get him to go out of the house, to pick up hobbies, to meet people, to take up sports – but to no avail. Both of Ron's parents were tired of him sitting at home all the time, never going out with his peers and always begging them to play games with him or just to keep him company. Ron's reason for behaving in this way, abnormal for a boy of his age, was that he was afraid of being bullied. He told them that in his own class at school nobody bullied him, but wherever else he went the bullying always started. What he meant by bullying was mostly name-calling and shouting. The kids in the neighbourhood where he lived, for example, called him 'The Nose' and did not hesitate to shout obscenities at him if he happened to pass by on his bicycle.

Ron did not imagine things, nor did he exaggerate. The bullying was real but there was no way for me to make it stop. I therefore suggested another course of action to Ron, to enable him to become so strong that he would be resistant to any kind of name-calling or shouting that might come his way.

Ron was not enthusiastic about my suggestion but he agreed to give it a try. I gave him a task for our next session. He was to go out as much as possible to get the neighbourhood kids to call him names and shout obscenities at him. The idea was that he would collect them and write them down in a notebook to show me at our next meeting. Ron did exactly as we had planned and when he came for his next appointment he showed me a long list of nasty names and other obscenities he had been subjected to during the previous week.

Together with Ron we came up with the following way in which he could practise his skill of not paying any attention to whatever was shouted at him. Ron was to imagine that he was wearing an invisible shield that made him invulnerable, the kind you see around the heroes of many computer games. When Ron gave me a sign that his shield was on, I read aloud to him things he had heard in the neighbourhood and recorded in his notebook. With the help of his imaginary shield, Ron quickly learned to take the nasty words I read to him with humour.

Gradually this skill of not paying any attention to teasing generalised to include other situations in his life. He found the courage to go out more and soon found a new sport that he liked a lot, and with that he began to get to know other young people and made many new friends.

Soiling

The word 'soiling' is often used to refer to children who are already mature enough to know how to defecate in the toilet but refuse to do it. They retain stools until they have an 'accident'.

Boyan Stahilov, a psychologist who teaches Kids' Skills in Bulgaria, has told me the following story:

I was invited to teach a Kids' Skills seminar in the old Bulgarian capital, Veliko Turnovo. In teaching seminars I usually see real cases. This time I met Daniela who works as a psychologist in the nearby SOS Children's Village. The Village is a home for children who have lost their parents for various reasons. Daniela had invited a nine-year-old boy called Jivko and his foster mother from the Children's Village to our seminar.

I greeted his foster mother and Jivko before we started the session. I learned that Jivko did not want to join us for the session so I agreed that he could stay in the next room drawing with the crayons his foster mother had brought along.

When we sat down the foster mother told us about Jivko's inability to control himself and to make it to the toilet quickly enough. She said the other children in the family had not noticed the problem yet, but she was afraid of their reactions when they found out. She feared they would tease him and reject him. The mother also told us that Jivko was new to her family, and had lived with them for only seven months. In addition to Jivko, she cared for four other foster children.

I then spoke a little about Kids' Skills, explaining its basic steps. Soon we were talking about the skill Jivko needed to learn: the skill of being able to make it to the toilet in time. The mother told us about the many obvious benefits this would have for the family as well as for Jivko himself. Above all, learning that skill would allow Jivko to play with other children instead of being rejected and having to play alone. The mother predicted that the skill would boost his self-esteem and it might even give him the status of a kind of 'leader of the pack'. An additional benefit was that it would allow Jivko to join the family for an excursion to Italy that was planned to take place the following month. When we discussed the idea of a celebration, the mother said that she would be willing to organise a party for Jivko even in the case of noticeable progress without full recovery. The consultation took an hour and ended with me wishing good luck to both mother and Jivko.

Comments by Jivko's foster mother:

When Jivko came to our SOS Village I immediately noticed that he soiled his underpants. At first I thought that it was just a temporary bad habit that would soon pass as he became used to being with us. However, after half a year with us he was well adapted but the problem persisted. I reserved an appointment with a paediatrician who examined Jivko and said that there was no physiological reason for it. I then went to see Daniela, who works as a psychologist in our Village. She suggested that we all go together to speak with Boyan who was teaching a seminar in town about solving children's problems.

My idea was to let Jivko talk about the problem with Boyan, but then Jivko refused. What could I do? I decided to talk with Boyan myself and we started by discussing what Jivko was good at, and about the things he had already learned. We spoke about Jivko's adaptation to our family group, and I described the things he had succeeded with. The meeting was brief but very useful for me. After it, we continued the work with Daniela. I did quite a few things myself. I encouraged and praised him a lot – and fortunately there was plenty of reason to do so. He was also very motivated himself because he really wanted to join us on our trip to Italy. Soon after the meeting with Boyan, Jivko started soiling less frequently and within four months the problem had disappeared completely. I succeeded in helping him keep up his self-confidence and status among the other children by directing them, too, to pay attention to Jivko's successes only.

Comments by Daniela, the psychologist at the Children's Village:

Jivko's mother came to talk with me about Jivko's inability to make it to the toilet quickly enough. I immediately thought about the possibility of inviting Jivko and his mother to join me for the Kids' Skills seminar, so that all of us could get some new ideas about what to do. The consultation at the seminar was pleasant and it became apparent to all of us that Jivko had many resources and abilities. For me the session was useful as it gave me the confidence to go on and use Kids' Skills in this case. Jivko's mother found the approach easy to accept. It was like a nice and exciting game. In fact, I later found out that some of the other children in the family group had been 'infected' with the ideas of Kids' Skills as well.

I met with Jivko several times after the seminar, not in my office where I usually see children, but in his own room. With hindsight, this appeared to have been a good decision. When we met we sat on the floor talking, drawing, playing, and having many good laughs.

The skill that Jivko wanted to learn was to be able to reach the toilet in time. I found it interesting that he wanted to draw a map, which showed the location of each toilet in our Village. Then he made plans about which one of them he should use depending on where he was at the time he would get 'the call'. Jivko started to make progress from day one. Even when we met the first time in his room, he could tell me some stories of success. When we examined the benefits of learning his skill he became interested in having a poster on his wall about his project. When he had learned his skill, and the problem was already in the past, Jivko asked all the other children in the family to help him in organising a party, which was held on the day of his tenth birthday.

Comments by Jivko himself:

The thing that I wanted most of all in the world was to cure myself. I had thought that this would never happen. Then I asked myself, 'Will I continue to do this or will I overcome this?' When Daniela asked me, 'When did you first realise that this was a problem you could overcome?' I remember my reply. I said, 'I realised it when I started to speak about it with my mother.' When we went to the workshop and I met Boyan I was embarrassed but I liked the two posters that I saw on the wall over there. I still remember the name of one of them. It was called 'The self-cured'. It had a picture of a boy with balloons. I made a similar poster for myself, too. I like drawing very much. Now things are as they sing in the [popular Bulgarian] song, 'I sing my heart out'.

Comments by Boyan Stahilov, the consultant:

Looking back I'd like to say that I did next to nothing. I was simply curious about whether Daniela and Jivko's mother would find the ideas of Kids' Skills useful. Jivko didn't want to join us and I had no problem with that. Instead of speaking with him, I spoke with his mother about what she could do to help him. For what happened after the consultation all credit goes to others, not to me – mainly to Jivko himself. This experience has left me with another assurance of the importance of having people around us to support us. I wish to thank Daniela, Jivko's mother and Jivko for the opportunity to tell this lovely example of Kids' Skills in action.

Horror at summer camp

The following story is about helping children overcome fears. It is not a description of a particular child having a particular fear, but about a group of children sharing the same fear.

Maiju Ahola, a primary school teacher who was working as an instructor on a summer camp for children aged seven to eleven, has contributed the story:

Our camp had just started when one of the older children in the group made up a story about there being a man in the outhouse [a primitive pit toilet] who sat down in the toilet hole smoking cigarettes. The smaller children took the story seriously and with their lively imaginations even added some details to the story. Before long the man had turned into a smoking white-haired monster that was stalking anybody coming to use the toilet.

The whole thing got out of hand and we soon had a case of full-blown toilet hysteria. Five girls were crying desperately in the yard, refusing to go anywhere near the outhouse building. We, the instructors, tried our best to calm them down. Among other things, we shone a flashlight down into the toilet hole to convince the children that there was no monster there. This approach, however, did not succeed in convincing the agitated children, who were positive they had seen something moving in the outhouse. Not surprisingly, at the same time the children began to talk about missing home.

The instructors got together for an emergency meeting to talk about what to do to calm the children down. I suggested that we try to do it with the help of Kids' Skills, and my colleagues thought it was a good idea. I gathered six of the crying girls together and told them, in a secretive voice, that I knew of a way in which we could get rid of the Outhouse Monster. I said that I had previous experience of monsters that like to come to harass children on camps. I also explained that it was possible to get rid of such monsters by combating them together. At this stage the crying had ended and the children listened to me attentively.

We then started to draw up a plan about how to slay the outhouse monster. While drawing the plan on a large sheet of paper, one of the children acted as a secretary. A couple of boys who joined us became excited about a 'slaying the monster' war. They volunteered to build traps to help catch the monster. I encouraged them by telling them that this too was a very good way of getting rid of monsters. I explained that for us to win the battle, we would need back-up forces. By back-up forces I meant power creatures that the children could wear around their necks as talismans. Our secretary wrote the word 'talismans' on our plan in big letters. In reality the talisman was a piece of cardboard hanging around the necks of children, onto which they had drawn a picture of their power creature. The power creature was supposed to protect the children and to give them the courage they needed to go to the outhouse to confront the monster. The children also gave names to their power creatures and wrote the names on their cards. The boys drew detailed plans about the monster traps they were going to construct.

More and more children gathered around the table. As the children who had not been affected by the hysteria noticed that plans were being made to start a battle against the outhouse monster, they too announced that they were afraid of the monster. This way they could join us in the making of power creature talismans. In the end there were no less than fifteen children around the table. Getting rid of the outhouse monster had turned into a fun and exciting game that everyone could participate in. The girls who just a moment before had cried in agitation were now matter-of-factly explaining to the newcomers what the challenge was that they were preparing to overcome.

We even made a plan about how we would celebrate when we had won the battle against the monster. It was agreed that we would have a victory toast together.

When the power creature cards were ready, we approached the outhouse. From the stairs we proclaimed the battle against the monster. This was a ceremony not unlike when a new bridge is opened. We solemnly cut a red cord that I had hung across the front of the outhouse. At the request of the children I gave a grand speech, at the end of which the children hung their power creatures around their necks.

Standing there on the steps of the outhouse you could sense the excitement and the fear of the children. As a person with experience in combating outhouse monsters, I promised to act as a personal bodyguard for them. As weapons I had two good-sized wooden spoons. I said that, if needed, I would use them to send the outhouse monster packing. This gave the children courage to start with the first exercise.

I wanted the children to progress with small steps. Together we approached the open door of the outhouse. Each child was to go in and quickly knock on the closed lid of the toilet. I showed them how. The first child was rewarded with a round of applause, which in turn encouraged the other children to step in and knock on the lid. The last one of the children was so brave and boisterous that he had the courage to lift the lid and take a quick peek under it. I asked him if he had seen the monster and he said he hadn't. After that all the children wanted to go in to take a peek under the lid. I praised them for their courage by shaking hands with all of them personally.

At the end of this first battle I promised to stay at the outhouse so that the children could safely go in and use the toilet. I knew that by now they must have needed the toilet desperately! When one of the children had succeeded in sitting on the toilet without anything strange taking place, there was a chain reaction: all the children found the courage to go to the toilet calmly. From then on the children were on their own, waging their own personal battles against the outhouse monster with the assistance of their power creatures. In addition, it was agreed that if one day somebody's power creature didn't show up, I would protect him or her with my wooden spoons when they needed to pay a visit to the outhouse.

That afternoon the boys demonstrated their imaginative outhouse monster traps to all the children. My colleague who had been with the boys said they had enjoyed the project immensely and they had done it responsibly. As lures, the boys used pine cones. The idea was that the monster would mistake the cones for bits of 'poo', and when it noticed that they were not poo, it would go mad and the box would fall over it. The boys showed us a few of these ingenious inventions and I documented all of them with my digital camera.

During that day a few of the girls came to tell me that they had visited the outhouse all by themselves, that they hadn't seen a trace of the monster and that they were no longer afraid of it. I drew a sign on their power creature cards to indicate that they had conquered the monster. The sign was an indication of the child's courage and also a deputation to act as a bodyguard for children who were still a bit afraid of the monster.

Before the sun went down the monster had been taken care of and the children, one after the other, asserted that they knew that outhouse monsters didn't even exist. After all, how could anybody smoke cigarettes in a smelly place like that!

A couple of days later, when the children were already getting ready to leave the camp to go back home, all the children who had participated in the battle against the outhouse monster got together and had a toast to celebrate their victory. Nice words were said about the other children in the camp for their support and for being examples of having the courage to go to the outhouse.

Tantrums

Tantrums are uncontrollable and prolonged bouts of anger. In a typical case, they start with the child experiencing a frustration or not getting her way. The child then gets angry and starts crying and yelling. The rage gradually grows and then gets out of hand. We can safely say that the child is no longer in control of her rage but that rage, instead, is in control of the child. Such a tantrum may last up to half an hour. After the tantrum the child is tired and may fall asleep from sheer exhaustion. In using Kids' Skills, we would want the child to learn the skills that children need to manage their frustrations.

Josée Lamarre, a psychologist from Quebec in French Canada, has told the following story:

This is the story of a six-year-old boy called Alexander, who had a bad temper. His parents had come to the conclusion that his tantrums came when he needed to do something that was hard for him and required effort. At school Alexander's temper was a significant issue because he used it as an excuse to refuse to try to do anything new that was demanding. At home, when it was time to do his homework after dinner, he would keep on doing other things with the result that his parents had to yell at him to get him to do what he was supposed to do for school.

Both the parents and the teacher were tired of the situation. It had got so bad that Alexander's refusal to do anything demanding was now even in the way of him learning to ride his bicycle without training wheels.

Alexander also had another issue: aggressive behaviour towards other children. When he got angry he would hit them, insult them, or spit in their faces. He needed to learn two skills: one was to learn to do things that required effort, and the other one was to be gentle and kind to his friends. I didn't know what to do because I didn't think he would be able to learn both skills at once. His parents wanted him to start with learning to handle school tasks that required effort so we decided we would start there.

When I met with Alexander I asked him if he wanted to learn the skill of doing tasks that required effort. He immediately said 'yes'. He gave the skill the name 'Super Mario', after the Nintendo hero who is always doing strenuous things. The advantages that Alexander saw in learning to do things that require effort was that he would be left with more time for playing. His parents told him about these advantages. They would be happier and they would praise him more often instead of constantly complaining about his behaviour. They also pointed out that the teacher would admire him at school and reward him with fun stickers for the homework that he had done.

Alexander chose Spider Man to be his power creature, or 'ami magique' as we say in French. He attached an image of Spider Man next to his bed and his teacher allowed him to attach another one on his desk to help him during lessons.

Alexander was convinced that he could live up to the challenge of learning the skill because he had already learned many difficult things in his life. His parents said that they believed he could do it because he had a lot of determination. Whenever he was onto something he would not easily give it up. The conclusion was that if Alexander decided to learn something, he would surely succeed.

Our next task was to figure out how Alexander could practise this skill. We came up with the idea that every evening, well before going to bed, he would practise doing homework that required effort for ten minutes. He would do it on his own, or with the help of one of his parents if he needed it. He was always to start by closing his eyes and repeating to himself three times: 'I am good'. Only after having said that was he to go on to doing the demanding homework.

When I saw Alexander a week later, I learned that he had improved a lot. I asked him how he had done it. He then explained to me that he had always done the 'I am good' ritual before starting the practice, and that he had also discovered another trick that had worked well for him. He had learned to concentrate his gaze on the sheet of paper he was using for his homework. I admired Alexander for his invention, as this was truly a great idea, taking into consideration that he had the tendency to be easily distracted by anything happening around him.

Alexander had done well at school. In his workbook there were lots of notes by the teacher about good behaviour. He even said that he had started to like going to school! At home he had done his homework – most of the time without any help from his parents – with the result that he actually had more time to play with his friends. He was very happy about that. Alexander and his parents left the session in a positive mood.

After one week Alexander's mother called me on the phone. She was very worried and told me that Alexander had attacked a child who had disturbed him in class while he had been doing something that required effort. We had an emergency meeting. I explained to Alexander that we were all facing a very difficult problem that could ruin our project if we didn't find a solution to it. The problem was that if Alexander had to be punished for his aggressive behaviour towards other children during the time he was doing his effort tolerance training, he might give up – and then he would never have all the benefits and advantages we had talked about. This would be a shame, I said, as he was being so successful.

I explained that in addition to learning to do demanding things, Alexander would also need to learn to be gentle towards other children. Then I shook my head sadly and said that learning two skills at once was too much to ask from a child. Alexander responded as I had hoped he would. He immediately announced that he could do it. He could learn two skills at once, to do things that required effort and to behave gently towards other children.

So we started to think about what skill he needed to develop to improve his behaviour towards other children. We came to the conclusion that he needed to learn to be gentle towards them, the way his cat Charlotte was gentle towards everyone. Hence the skill was named 'Charlotte'. We started to examine what this skill meant in practice.

From the examples of tough situations with other children that Alexander told me about, I understood that he needed to learn to defend himself verbally, instead of using his fists to defend himself when other children said things to him that he did not like. For example, when a little girl had told him at lunch that he should eat the crust of his bread, he had scratched her face instead of saying something to her. When I asked him what else he could do instead of scratching a child the next time something like that happened, he said he did not know. I suggested that he could say the words, 'Mind your own business'. Alexander thought this was a great idea. We role-played a number of situations where I said something unkind to him and he practised verbal self-defence. I also suggested that his parents reserve five minutes every evening to practise verbal self-defence with him. The parent would say something unkind to Alexander and he was to respond verbally rather than physically. It was like a game and it was a lot of fun, too.

At our next meeting I learned that Alexander had improved a lot on both battlefronts. His reputation at school was getting better, and he liked going to school more and more. His parents had been so happy with his progress that they had taken him out to eat at a restaurant and they had been in such a good mood that they had played games with him. The rest of the session was spent planning for the celebration. Alexander invited some friends to his party, as well as his grandparents who had been good supporters all along. The food he wanted to serve was hot dogs and chips. The party was a great success.

What I learned from working with Alexander was that if children really want to, they can learn two skills at once.

Starting fires

The following story is about a ten-year-old boy, whose issue was playing with matches. In this case, it was far from an innocent game because the boy had already started two real fires that the fire brigade had had to put out. This case study was presented many years ago, with video clips from actual sessions, at a family therapy conference by Jay Haley, one of the foremost pioneers of the family therapy movement. I will try to replicate the story here, in my own words, because I think it is an outstanding illustration of the idea that children can overcome problems by learning skills.

Let's say the boy's name was Don. The father, mother and Don were sitting in the appointment room with the therapist. They were in a gloomy mood as they talked about what had happened. The therapist left the room to consult the other members of the treatment team who were observing the session from behind a one-way mirror. When he came back he turned to Don and said: 'You know, Don, you are really lousy at handling fire. You don't seem to know the slightest thing about how to handle it. No wonder you can't control fire!'

Don was baffled. He had probably been expecting to be scolded once again for the things he had done with matches but now, to his surprise, he was scolded for not knowing how to handle fire. The therapist brought back some things from the other room and then placed them on the table in front of the family. They included a metal container, some paper and a box of matches.

'OK, Don, now let's see what you can do,' the therapist said, and handed Don the matches. 'I want you to light this piece of paper and to burn it in this container. Your parents and I will observe you to see how you do it.'

Don surely wondered what this was all about but he did as he was told. He took the piece of paper in his hand, lit it with a match and let it burn in the metal container. When he was done, the therapist said: 'Let me be honest with you, Don. That was a lousy performance. I can point out to you all the cardinal mistakes that you made. First of all, you struck the match in the wrong direction, secondly you lit the paper while you held it – you should have done that while the paper was in the container – and thirdly, you didn't keep your eyes constantly on the fire but kept looking here and there while the paper was burning. This demonstration proves I'm right. You're a slob when it comes to handling fire and you urgently need to learn to become better at it to make sure that nothing like this ever happens again.'

The therapist then proposed – in this case, you might say ordered – that Don's father start to coach him, on a daily basis, in the art of handling fire. It was by no means coincidental that the therapist picked Don's father to function as his coach. What Don had been doing had practically ruined the father–son relationship and the therapist saw this as an opportunity for healing their bond.

Both Don and his father went along with the therapist's proposal. The remaining time in the session was used to discuss various ways in which Don's father could teach his son the art of handling fire over the next two weeks. The father was to teach Don such skills as how to light a charcoal grill, how to safely light and extinguish a campfire outdoors, how various materials burn, how a fire extinguisher works, and more.

When the therapist next met with Don and his parents, Don had made a lot of progress. With his father's coaching he had learned many things and he was already quite knowledgeable about fire and the handling of it, surely much more knowledgeable than other children of his age. As a side effect of the training, the relationship between Don and his father had improved considerably. There was some reason to believe that Don had already overcome his life-threatening obsession with fire but the therapist wanted to play it safe. He ordered Don and his father to continue to practise the art of handling fire for another two weeks.

When the family came for the next session, Don was so fed up with studying fire safety that he suggested that between then and the next session he be allowed to do something else with his father.

Through practising the art of handling fire safely, Don learned a skill that he urgently needed. At the same time his relationship with his father became warmer. This side effect, an improvement in the child–parent relationship, is characteristic of any successful approach to helping children – including Kids' Skills. When parents are allowed an active role in helping their children, it inevitably has a favourable effect on their relationship.

Attention Deficit Hyperactive Disorder (ADHD)

Attention Deficit Disorder and the often-accompanying hyperactivity is a commonly diagnosed condition in children. It is thought that it is caused by an abnormality, or immaturity, in how the child's brain processes information. Kids' Skills lends itself well to treating this condition. However, to use this approach we should think of the disturbance not as a single entity but as a combination of related problems, each of which can be solved separately by converting it into a skill the child can learn.

For example, a child with ADHD might have the following symptoms: constant moving around and inability to sit still; constantly interrupting other people; difficulty in waiting for anything that doesn't happen immediately; and distractability, being easily sidetracked from any task by the slightest sound or movement nearby.

When using Kids' Skills we would view this child simply as a child with several skills he needs to learn or to improve. For example, in this particular case the child would need to

- learn to sit still

- learn to ask for a turn to speak

- learn to wait patiently for things

- learn to concentrate on a task even when there are disturbances around.

In fact, helping ADHD children with the Kids' Skills approach does not differ in any way from helping children without this condition. Whether the cause of the lack of a particular skill is psychological or neurological is not of great significance in Kids' Skills. The approach is as well suited for developing skills related to problems with a neurological basis as it is for developing skills typically conceived of as psychological. We simply identify the specific symptoms of ADHD, convert them into skills to be learned, and then help the child learn those skills one by one. Here we may, however, want to remember the idea of *small steps*. For example, for some ADHD children the skill of being able to sit still or to play alone for five minutes is already quite a feat.

Jim was a five-year-old boy with ADHD at Keula Day Care Centre. He was not taking psychostimulant medication as this form of treatment is still relatively rarely used in Finland. Jim was a lovable boy, always in a good mood. Yet he was quite a nuisance because of his hyperactivity and 'wild' behaviour. When Jim came to Keula, one his most disturbing behaviours was his peculiar manner of greeting people – adults as well as his peers. He would joyfully greet people by punching them in the back with his fist, or by jumping onto them out of the blue as if he wanted to be carried piggyback. There was no intention to hurt anyone; the behaviour was rather a consequence of clumsiness and hyperactivity. Other issues included Jim's stacking too much food on his plate and devouring too much food too fast, so that after lunch he often suffered from stomach ache and flatulence. Needless to say, another issue he had was the inability to sit still or to stay in one place for more than a minute or so. Due to his impulsivity Jim was actually dangerous to other children.

The first skill Jim learned at the day care centre was the skill of greeting people in a socially appropriate way. This skill included initiating the greeting by establishing eye contact, then shaking hands and saying something friendly such as 'Hi, Johnny' or 'Hello, Ms Ruttner'. Jim learned this skill in a few weeks and was ready to move on to learning the next skill, which was becoming better at estimating how much food he needed and then eating the portion unhurriedly. During the two-year period Jim was at the centre he learned quite a few skills, including that of sitting still for more than five minutes. With the help of the skills he acquired at Keula he did well at school despite his condition.

Bringing it all together

If you have read through the whole book, by now you will know the fifteen steps of Kids' Skills quite well, and you will also understand how they can be applied. We can now bring together all that we have learned:

- Kids' Skills is an educational tool and a problem-solving method with which we can help children overcome problems by learning new skills. This approach is based on the idea that children should actively participate in learning the skills they need to overcome difficulties.

- To use this method we first have to identify a skill or ability which, when mastered, will lead to the removal of the problem.

- We then agree with the child that he will start to learn the particular skill, making sure he understands what having that skill means in practice.

- So that the child will truly want to learn the skill, we help her become aware of the benefits of having this skill, for herself as well as others. We also boost her motivation by together planning a celebration for the time when she has gained mastery of the skill.

- For the child to start learning the skill, he needs to have confidence that he can succeed in learning it. We can help build the child's confidence by letting him have a power creature that will help him learn, by encouraging him to recruit a good number of supporters, and by letting him hear why people are confident he will succeed in learning the skill.

- For the child to have the motivation and the energy to practise her skill, we must make sure the child enjoys rehearsing the skill by giving her generous praise and positive feedback for any signs of progress.

- To safeguard against possible setbacks having a demoralising effect, we must prepare the child to deal with them by letting him tell us how he wants other people to help him if and when he loses his skill.

- A newly learned skill needs to be reinforced for it to become a habit rather than something one can only do consciously. Therefore arrange for the child to have an opportunity to celebrate learning the skill and to acknowledge all those people who contributed, in one way or another, to her learning it. In addition, try to arrange for her to have an opportunity to teach her skill to someone else and, finally, let her start learning another skill.

- Kids' Skills is primarily a method with which we can help children overcome problems and learn skills. However, the beneficial effects of this method are not limited to the child alone, but extend to the child's environment as well. When the people around the child join forces to help the child learn important skills, it helps them become better parents and caregivers for the child. This in turn creates not only a nurturing environment in which children can thrive, but a happier and more positive community.

Difficulties and obstacles are an inherent part of the lives of children. How we think about problems, and how we try to resolve them, has an extensive influence not only on our own personal wellbeing but also the wellbeing of our children.

If we consider our children's issues to be psychological or emotional disturbances, approach them as something to be ashamed of, talk about them behind closed doors, and hand the solving of them on to experts, there is a risk that we will feel incompetent and unable to help our own children. Then our children, in turn, become convinced that there is something wrong with them, something that is beyond their own control.

If, on the other hand, instead of seeing problems we see the skills or abilities our children need to learn or refine, we can reclaim our faith in ourselves as parents or educators, and in our ability to teach our children to understand that problems are part and parcel of life, and that they can best be overcome when people help and support each other.

Acknowledgements

First of all I want to warmly thank all those children, fathers, mothers, teachers, educators and professional helpers I have encountered over the years who have helped me to create an understanding of how to help children overcome difficulties.

Even if I am officially the author of this book, it doesn't mean that I have invented Kids' Skills by myself: Kids' Skills is the product of teamwork. The other members of the team include Tapani Ahola, my colleague, and special education teachers Tuija Terävä and Sirpa Birn.

The philosophy behind Kids' Skills has also not come out of the blue: its roots are in the international brief therapy movement. The influence of the following innovators in the field is particularly apparent in Kids' Skills:

- **Milton H. Erickson** (1902–1980), American psychiatrist and the pioneer of modern brief therapy. Please visit the website of the Milton H. Erickson Foundation at *www.erickson-foundation.org* to find out more about this extraordinary man.

- **Insoo Kim Berg** and **Steve De Shazer,** who have been central figures in the development of the solution-focused approach to brief therapy. You can find out more about applying solution-focused therapy to children's issues by getting hold of the excellent book by Insoo Kim Berg and Therese Steiner, *Children's solutions work,* published by Norton, New York 2002. For more information visit the website of the Brief Family Therapy Centre at *www.brief-therapy.org*.

- **David Epston** from New Zealand and **Michael White** from Australia, who have been instrumental in the birth of an approach to brief therapy called narrative therapy. You can find a wealth of examples of the application of this approach to problem-solving with children in the charming book by Jennifer Freeman, David Epston and Dean Lobovits, *Playful approaches to serious problems,* published by Norton, New York 1997. Also consider visiting *www.narrativeapproaches.com* to learn more.

- **Cloé Madanes,** a renowned American family therapist and one of the originators of what has been called strategic brief therapy. You will find information about her creative ideas in her books, *Behind the one-way mirror* and *Strategic family therapy,* published by Jossey Bass, San Francisco 1984 and 1981. Find out more about Cloé Madanes at her own website *www.cloemadanes.com.*

This book has been made possible by all those people who have contributed by submitting stories about their experiences using Kids' Skills, either with the children they work with or with their own children. I would like to warmly thank the following people for their contributions: Tuija Terävä, Sirpa Birn, Katja Furman, Maiju Ahola, Elise Luovula (Finland); Alfred Bratterud, Ivar Haug (Norway); Josée Lamarre (Canada); Boyan Stahilov (Bulgaria); Hooshmand Ebrahimi (Iran); Lisa Brennan (Ireland); Viveka Grut Lilieros (Sweden); and Andrew Duggan, Anne Turner (Great Britain).

The word about Kids' Skills has spread around the world with astonishing speed. Originally the approach was called *Muksuoppi* in Finnish. In English we decided to call it *Kids' Skills.* Some of the other translations are: *Jag Kan* in Swedish; *Jeg Kan!* in Norwegian; *Ich Schaff's* in German; *Ik kan het* in Dutch; and *Je suis capable* in French.

The following people have helped spread the word about Kids' Skills in the countries where they work: Hooshmand Ebrahimi (Iran); Andrew Duggan (Great Britain); Tom Hegeman, Manfred Vogt-Hillman, Wolfgang Burr, (Germany); Susanne Heincz, Veronika Schöffl (Austria); Karin Walgren, Viveka Grut Lilieros, Stefan Görson (Sweden); Ivar Haug and Netverket SFO (Norway); Brief Therapy Partners, Lisa Brennan (Ireland); Hans Mulder, Bert and Margriet Hamense (Netherlands); Josée Lamarre, André Grégoire (Canada); Boyan Stahilov (Bulgaria); Jacek Lelonkiewicz (Poland); Bob Bertolino, Belinda Willis, Frank Thomas (USA); Michael Durrant, St Luke's Innovative Resources (Australia); Henrik Petersen (Denmark); and Annette Mainz (Kurdistan).

Kids' Skills Tools

Kids' Skills Website

A wealth of information about Kids' Skills and related products can be found at the official Kids' Skills website **www.kidsskills.org.**

The following materials are available directly from Innovative Resources in Australia:

St Luke's Innovative Resources
137 McCrae Street
BENDIGO VIC 3050 Australia
Phone 03 5442 0500 International +61 3 5442 0500
Fax 03 5442 0555 International +61 3 5442 0555
info@innovativeresources.org
www.innovativeresources.org

Kids' Skills Handbook

Kids' Skills is a problem-solving method for children based on solution-focused educational psychology. This method helps children learn skills, solve problems, and transform undesired behaviours. At the heart of this material is the notion that practically all children's problems can be seen as skills that the child needs to learn or improve.

Kids' Skills does not blame children or parents for the child's difficulties. Instead, it invites parents to actively participate in each of the stages of the process. The Kids' Skills Handbook is the first English translation of this practical and effective approach.

Kids' Skills Workbook

A twenty-four-page illustrated workbook with a spread for each step of the Kids' Skills process. The Workbook is a notebook for writing down everything that you agree on with the child. In addition there is a page in the Workbook where the supporters are asked to write words of support and encouragement. When Kids' Skills is used at school, the Workbook facilitates school–parent communication and cooperation. It also serves as a means for going public and telling people about the child's learning project.

Kids' Skills Video

An educational video about Kids' Skills, in English. In this video Dr Ben Furman takes you through the fifteen steps of Kids' Skills. In addition you will see the British child therapist Andrew Duggan interviewing staff, children and parents at the Keula preschool (Finland) where Kids' Skills was originally developed, plus clips from a family session in England where Andrew is using the method to help a child overcome the habit of lying. Duration 30 minutes.

Some useful references

Insoo Kim Berg & Therese Steiner
Children's solutions work
Norton, New York 2002

Michael Durrant
Creative strategies for school problems
Norton, New York 1995

Jennifer Freeman, David Epston & Dean Lobovits
Playful approaches to serious problems
Norton, New York 1997

Ben Furman
Never too late to have a happy childhood:
from adversity to resiliency
BT Press, London 1998

Ben Furman & Tapani Ahola
Solution talk: hosting therapeutic conversations
Second edition
BT Press, London 2001

Linda Metcalf
Teaching toward solutions: step-by-step strategies for
handling academic, behaviour and family issues in the classroom
The Centre for Applied Research and Education, New York 1994

Matthew D. Selekman
Solution-focused therapy with children:
harnessing family strengths for systemic change
Guilford, New York 1997